Of the imitation of Christ, four books, the Thomas à Kempis. The 'Edith Cavell' ed., with an introd. by Herbert E. Ryle

Anonymous

The World's Classics

XLIX

OF THE

IMITATION OF CHRIST

THE 'EDITH CAVELL' EDITION

Arrested 5 June, 1915?
Prison de la filles 7 May, 1915
Court-martialled 7th Oct 1915
8 " "
Condemned to death 8 Oct
In the Salle des deputies   at 10.30 am
with others. (The accused numbered (in all)
in all 70. Of whom 34 were present
or their 2 dit ?
Died at 7 a.m on Oct 12th 1915

E Cavell

with love to

E E Cavell

OF THE
IMITATION OF
CHRIST

FOUR BOOKS

BY

THOMAS À KEMPIS

THE 'EDITH CAVELL' EDITION

WITH AN INTRODUCTION BY

THE RIGHT REV. BISHOP HERBERT
E. RYLE, D.D., C.V.O.
Dean of Westminster

HUMPHREY MILFORD
OXFORD UNIVERSITY PRESS
LONDON EDINBURGH GLASGOW
NEW YORK TORONTO MELBOURNE CAPE TOWN
BOMBAY CALCUTTA AND MADRAS

Thomas Haemmerlein (à Kempis)
 Born: Kempen, Germany, 1380.
 Died: Zwolle, July 23, 1471.

The first edition of 'The Imitation of Christ' ap-
 peared in Latin in the year 1470 circ., and the
 first English translation in 1677. It was first
 published in 'The World's Classics' in the year
 1903, and reprinted in 1906 and 1909 and the
 'Edith Cavell' edition twice in 1920.

TO
QUEEN ALEXANDRA,
TO WHOSE GRACIOUS INTEREST
AND ENCOURAGEMENT
THE HOMES OF REST FOR NURSES,
ESTABLISHED
IN MEMORY OF
THE SUPREME SACRIFICE OF
NURSE EDITH CAVELL,
OWE SO MUCH.

FOREWORD BY BISHOP RYLE

Reader,

You have here a rare treasure. This little edition of the *Imitation of Christ* is a facsimile of the copy which belonged to Edith Cavell, and which she had with her in the prison of St.-Gilles in Brussels. Two months intervened between her arrest on August 5, 1915, and her court-martial on October 7 and 8. The cruel sentence of death was announced to her on the afternoon of October 11: she was executed at 7 a.m. on October 12, 1915.

During the long lonely period of her imprisonment, as well as during the last three days of dreadful expectancy, she used this little book. You can see reproduced in these pages the markings that she made at different times against passages which she found especially helpful and comforting. You will find there are about sixty of these markings. They have been made at different times. The same pen is not used: the character of the markings varies. Sometimes the lines are long and thin; sometimes short and clumsy; sometimes there are two or three lines in the margin of a single short sentence.

You will find these marked passages in the following pages: 1, 2, 5, 7, 17, 18, 21, 22, 26, 29, 31, 35, 36, 44, 45, 49, 50, 51, 52, 54, 55, 58, 59, 60, 61, 62, 63, 71, 72, 76, 82, 83, 86, 87, 88, 96, 100, 103, 104, 105, 108, 110, 118, 120, 121, 122, 124, 125, 126, 135, 136, 137, 153, 186, 191, 192, 199, 200, 201, 205.

In a few instances, she has written the date. When the date is given, it is October, 1915. Evidently she

was using this little book, and finding consolation
from it during the last days and hours of her life.
Thus, there are two crosses in ink, and the note
'St.-Gilles Oct. 1915', written at the head of two
successive chapters : chap. xxix 'How we ought to
call upon God, and to bless Him, when tribulation is
upon us', and chap. xxx 'Of craving the Divine Aid,
and Confidence of recovering Grace' (pp. 125, 126).

Towards the end of the *Imitation* there is a section
upon the 'Comfort of Devout Communion' (chap.
iv, p. 198). You will see that on page 200 Edith
Cavell has heavily marked a particular passage, and
written against it 'St.-Gilles 11 Oct.' This was the
day on which she was told at 4.30 p.m. that she was to
be executed, and that she was to be shot early next
morning. That evening, for the first time since her
arrest, she was allowed to see the English chaplain
(she had previously only been permitted to see the
German military chaplain: and she did not know
German). The English chaplain gave her the Holy
Communion at 10 p.m.

How full of sacred tenderness, then, is the confession
she has marked : 'I indeed labour in the sweat of my
brows. I am racked with grief of heart, I am burdened
with sins, I am troubled with temptations, I am entangled and oppressed with many evil passions; and
there is none to help me, none to deliver and save me,
but Thou O Lord God my Saviour, to whom I commit
myself and all that is mine, that Thou mayest keep
watch over me, and bring me safe to life everlasting'
(p. 200).

On page 205, in the chapter on 'Self-Examination
before Communion', she marked these two sentences:

' Then with full resignation and with thy entire will, offer up thyself to the honour of My Name, on the altar of thy heart, a perpetual whole burnt offering, even thy body and soul, faithfully committing them unto Me.'

' And when a man shall have done what lieth in him, and shall be truly penitent, how often soever he shall come to Me for pardon and grace, " as I live ", saith the Lord, " who will not the death of a sinner, but rather that he be converted and live, I will not remember his sins any more, but they shall all be forgiven him."'

In connexion with these marked passages we read with intense interest the official report by Mr. Gahan, British chaplain in Brussels :

' On Monday evening, October 11, I was admitted by special passport from the German authorities to the prison of St.-Gilles, where Miss Edith Cavell had been confined for ten weeks. The final sentence had been given early that afternoon.

' To my astonishment and relief I found my friend perfectly calm and resigned. But this could not lessen the tenderness and intensity of feeling on either part during that last interview of almost an hour.

' Her first words to me were upon a matter concerning herself personally, but the solemn asseveration which accompanied them was made expressedly in the light of God and eternity. She then added that she wished all her friends to know that she willingly gave her life for her country, and said : " I have no fear nor shrinking ; I have seen death so often that it is not strange or fearful to me." She further said : " I thank God for this ten weeks' quiet before the end." " Life has always been hurried and full of difficulty." "This time of rest has been a great mercy." "They have all been very kind to me here. But this I would say, standing as I do in view of God and eternity : I realize that patriotism is not enough. I must have no hatred or bitterness toward any one."

'We partook of the Holy Communion together, and she received the Gospel message of consolation with all her heart. At the close of the little service I began to repeat the words " Abide with me ", and she joined softly in the end.

'We sat quietly talking until it was time for me to go. She gave me parting messages for relations and friends. She spoke of her soul's needs at the moment, and she received the assurance of God's Word as only the Christian can do.

'Then I said " Good-bye ", and she smiled and said, "We shall meet again ".

'The German military chaplain was with her at the end and afterwards gave her Christian burial. He told me : " She was brave and bright to the last. She professed her Christian faith and that she was glad to die for her country." "She died like a heroine."

'H. STIRLING T. GAHAN,
'British Chaplain, Brussels.'[1]

Of the other passages which she has marked, it may be noticed that she evidently was keenly conscious of the evil done by indiscreet speech and idle gossip. One

[1] *Belgium under German Occupation*, by Brand Whitlock, vol. ii, p. 40. Heinemann, 1919. This and the other passages here quoted from the same book are reprinted by kind permission of Mr. William Heinemann, the publisher.

rumour was current to the effect that her arrest was due to the repetition by thoughtless friends of words which she had spoken in confidence. At the court-martial her entire truthfulness and her frank admission of what she had done for her countrymen and for Belgians furnished the German military authorities with the most serious charges against her. Notice then the emphasis with which she has marked such passages as these :

'O God, who art the truth, make me one with Thee in everlasting charity' (p. 5).

'Often take counsel in temptations, and deal not roughly with him that is tempted ; but give him comfort, as thou wouldest wish to be done to thyself' (p. 17).

'No man speaks securely, but he that holds his peace willingly' (p. 29).

'It were more just that thou shouldest accuse thyself, and excuse thy brother' [conspicuously marked in the margin, 'St.-Gilles' (p. 54)].

'It is no small prudence to keep silence in an evil time, and inwardly to turn thyself to Me, and not to be troubled by the judgment of men. Let not thy peace be in the tongues of men ; for whether they interpret well or ill of thee thou art not therefore another man' (p. 124).

We should compare with these passages the words (translated from her own French) in the farewell letter she wrote on October 10, 1915, to the members of the Training School for Nurses in Brussels, of which she had been the head and organizer since September 17, 1907.

'. . . To my regret I have not been able always to speak very much with you personally ; you know that

I have had a good many occupations, but I hope that you will not forget our evening chats. I told you that devotion would give you real happiness—and the thought that before God and yourselves you have done your entire duty with a good heart will be your greatest comfort in the hard moments of life and in the face of death.

'There are two or three of you who will recall the little interviews that we have had together; do not forget them Being already so far along in life, I have been able perhaps to see more clearly than you and to show you the straight path. One word more. Beware of gossip! And may I say to you—loving your country with all my heart—that'that is the great fault here? I have seen so much evil during these eight years that could have been avoided or lessened if there had not been a little word whispered here and there, perhaps not with malicious intention—but it ruined the reputation and happiness, even the life of some one. My nurses should think of that and cultivate among themselves loyalty and *esprit de corps*.

'If there is one among you whom I have wronged, I beg you to forgive me; I have been perhaps too severe sometimes, but never voluntarily unjust, and I have loved you all much more than you thought.

'My best wishes for the happiness of all my girls, those who have left the school as well as those who are there still, and thank you for the kindness that you have always shown me.

                                  'Your devoted directress,
  Oct. 10, 1915,   'EDITH CAVELL.'
      Prison of St.-Gilles.[1]

                ¹ Whitleck, *ibid.*, vol. ii, p. 44.

It only remains to call attention to a few other passages which seem more especially to have appealed to her.

'Occasions of adversity best discover how great virtue or strength each one hath. For occasions do not make a man frail, but they shew what he is' (p. 22).

'Thou must pass through fire and water before thou come to the place of refreshing' (p. 36).

'Put all thy trust in God, let Him be thy fear, and thy love: He shall answer for thee, and will do in all things what is best for thee' (p. 50).

'To glory in tribulation, is no hard thing for him that loveth; for so to glory, is to glory in the Cross of the Lord' (p. 58).

'Be thou humble and peaceable, and Jesus will be with thee. Be devout and quiet, and Jesus will stay with thee' (p. 61).

'That . . . I may be made fit to love, courageous to suffer, steady to persevere' (p. 83).

'My son, cast thy heart firmly on the Lord, and fear not the judgment of men, when conscience testifieth of thy dutifulness and innocency' (p. 137).

No more wonderful national tribute has ever been paid than that which was paid to Edith Cavell on the occasion of the great funeral service on May 15, 1919, in Westminster Abbey. The streets leading to the Abbey were lined by dense masses of people, bareheaded, silent, reverent. The little *cortège* consisted of the gun-carriage bearing the coffin covered with the Union Jack, and escorted by a single officer and a company of Grenadier Guards. Windows, roofs, parapets, were thronged with people. The Abbey itself was filled from end to end more than half an hour before the service began. Queen Alexandra was there as Patron of the Edith Cavell Homes of Rest for Nurses. Every nursing institution in the kingdom seemed to have representatives. Every part of the British Empire had sent contingents.

The journey to Norwich, where the remains were interred, called forth a no less remarkable demonstration. The special train was greeted by throngs who stood in the stations. School children crowded together at the level crossings to watch it pass. Men in khaki stood at attention. Workmen in the fields doffed their caps. All East Anglia seemed determined to do homage to the quiet, brave, devoted woman who had willingly died for her country, and whose body was to be laid to rest in the peaceful precincts of the Cathedral of Norwich.

She had been cruelly put to death. Hers was one of the great resolute sacrifices of the war. Her name will live in history. God heard her prayer, and gave her 'strength to resist, patience to endure, and constancy to persevere' (p. 121).

The time will come when people will ask, Who was Edith Cavell? and, Why was she put to death? All can now answer such inquiries. But memories are short: and the younger generation will quickly grow up, and will not have heard who she was, or what she did, or why she suffered.

I therefore subjoin two extracts from the important contemporary book *Belgium under German Occupation* (see note, page x) by His Excellency Brand Whitlock, United States Minister in Belgium, and resident in

Brussels from the beginning of the Great War in August 1914 until April 1917.

'Edith Cavell herself did not expect such a fate. She was a frail and delicate little woman about forty years of age. She had come to Brussels some years before to exercise her calling as a trained nurse, and soon became known to the leading physicians of the capital and nursed in the homes of the leading families. But she was ambitious and devoted to her profession, and ere long had entered a nursing-home in the Rue de la Clinique, where she organized for Dr. Depage a training school for nurses. She was a woman of refinement and education; she knew French well; she was deeply religious, with a conscience almost Puritan, and was very stern with herself in what she conceived to be her duty. In her training school she showed great executive ability, was firm in matters of discipline, and brought it to a high state of efficiency. And every one who knew her in Brussels spoke of her with that unvarying respect which her noble character inspired' (vol. ii, p. 10).

'Miss Cavell did not know, or knew only in the vaguest manner, the offence with which she was charged. No written statement of it had ever been delivered to her, no written statement of it had ever been given to her attorney, and it is a pathetic circumstance that it was her own honesty and frankness, her own direct English way of thinking, that convicted her. With the *naïveté* of the pure in heart she assumed that the Germans were charging her with the deeds that she had committed, and these she readily admitted, and even signed a paper to that effect. We know enough to be able to say that Miss Cavell did not deny having received at her hospital English soldiers, whom she nursed and to whom she gave money; she did not deny that she knew they were going to try to cross the border into Holland. She even took a patriotic pride in the fact. She was interrogated in German, a language she did not understand, but the questions and responses were translated into French. Her mind was alert, she was entirely calm and self-possessed, and frequently rectified inexact details in the statements that were put to her. When, in her interrogatory, she was asked if she had not aided English soldiers left behind after the early battles of the preceding autumn about Mons and Charleroi, she said yes; they were English and she was English, and she would help her own. The answer seemed to impress the court. They asked her if she had not helped twenty.

'"Yes," she said, "more than twenty; two hundred."

'" English?"

'"No, not all English; French and Belgians too."

But the French and Belgians were not of her own nationality, said the judge—and that made a serious difference. She was subjected to a nagging interrogatory. One of the judges said that she had been foolish to aid English soldiers, because the English are ungrateful.

'"No," replied Miss Cavell, "the English are not ungrateful."

'"How do you know they are not?" asked the inquisitor.

'"Because", she answered, "some of them have written to me from England to thank me."

'It was a fatal admission on the part of the tortured little woman; under the German military law her having helped soldiers to reach Holland, a neutral country, would have been a less serious offence, but to aid them to reach an enemy country, and especially England, was the last offence in the eyes of a German military court.'[1]

It only remains for me to explain how this book comes to be published. It appears that in her last moments Edith Cavell desired that her precious little copy of the *Imitation* should after her death be sent to her favourite cousin, Mr. E. D. Cavell. That gentleman never received it until October 1918, three years later, and then through the kindly and considerate action of the American Embassy.

To Mr. Cavell she had written, on March 11, 1915, the last letter of hers which was to reach England. She speaks in it of the time long ago when they were children : ' We were young', she says, ' and life was fresh and beautiful, and the country so desirable and sweet.' She speaks of her mother: ' The last letter from my Mother was date 22nd Jan. If this reaches you, will you send her a line to say all is well here? She is naturally very anxious, and I do not know whether she gets my letters. There are not many opportunities of sending.'

She spent part of the last evening of her life in writing to her mother. The German authorities refused to allow the letter to be sent. Mrs. Cavell passed away without having heard more than that her daughter had been executed at Brussels by the German military government.

Mr. E. D. Cavell courteously writes to me in the

[1] Whitlock, *ibid.*, vol. ii, pp. 11-13.

following terms: 'My object in allowing the publication of my Cousin's book is to increase the circulation of the writings of Thomas à Kempis and to assist the Homes of Rest by the proceeds of the sale.'

Reader, let us once more turn to the pages of the *Imitation*, and once more ponder over the sweet secret of a holy humble life, spent in the Saviour's service. This copy is fragrant with the prayer of a good English woman, lonely, in sore trouble, and with violent death imminent. May we find what Edith Cavell here found, the unspeakable comfort of the Divine Love of the Crucified Christ, commended and assured to us in the tender simple sentences of this most famous and precious book of Christian Devotion!

HERBERT E. RYLE,
Bishop.

The Deanery,
Westminster.
Armistice Day, November 11, 1919.

CONTENTS

THE FIRST BOOK

ADMONITIONS, USEFUL FOR A SPIRITUAL LIFE

THE SECOND BOOK

ADMONITIONS TENDING TO THINGS INTERNAL

THE THIRD BOOK

OF INTERNAL CONSOLATION

CONTENTS

CONTENTS

THE FOURTH BOOK

CONCERNING THE SACRAMENT

CONTENTS

OF THE IMITATION OF CHRIST

THE FIRST BOOK

ADMONITIONS, USEFUL FOR A SPIRITUAL LIFE

CHAPTER I

OF THE IMITATION OF CHRIST, AND CONTEMPT OF ALL THE VANITIES OF THE WORLD

'HE that followeth Me, walketh not in darkness,'[1] saith the Lord. These are the words of Christ, by which we are admonished how we ought to imitate His life and manners, if we will be truly enlightened, and be delivered from all blindness of heart.

Let therefore our chiefest endeavour be, to meditate upon the life of Jesus Christ.

II. The doctrine of Christ exceedeth all the doctrines of holy men ; and he that hath the Spirit, will find therein an hidden manna.

But it falleth out, that many who often hear the Gospel of Christ, are yet but little affected, because they are void of the Spirit of Christ.

But whosoever would fully and feelingly understand the words of Christ, must endeavour to conform his life wholly to the life of Christ.

III. What will it avail thee to dispute profoundly of the Trinity, if thou be void of humility, and art thereby displeasing to the Trinity?

---

[1] John viii. [12].

Surely high words do not make a man holy and just; but a virtuous life maketh him dear to God.

I had rather feel compunction, than understand the definition thereof.

If thou didst know the whole Bible by heart, and the sayings of all the philosophers, what would all that profit thee without the love of God [1] and without grace?

Vanity of vanities, and all is vanity,[2] except to love God, and to serve Him only.

This is the highest wisdom, by contempt of the world to tend towards the kingdom of Heaven.

IV. Vanity therefore it is to seek after perishing riches, and to trust in them.

It is also vanity to hunt after honours, and to climb to high degree.

It is vanity to follow the desires of the flesh, and to labour for that for which thou must afterwards suffer grievous punishment.

Vanity it is, to wish to live long, and to be careless to live well.

It is vanity to mind only this present life, and not to foresee those things which are to come.

It is vanity to set thy love on that which speedily passeth away, and not to hasten thither where everlasting joy abideth.

V. Call often to mind that proverb, 'The eye is not satisfied with seeing, nor the ear filled with hearing.'[3]

Endeavour therefore to withdraw thy heart from the love of visible things, and to turn thyself to the invisible.

For they that follow their sensuality, do stain their own consciences, and lose the favour of God.

---

[1] 1 Cor. xiii. [2].   [2] Eccles. i. [2].   [3] Eccles. i. [8].

CHAPTER II

OF THE HUMBLE CONCEIT OF OURSELVES

ALL men naturally desire to know ;[1] but what availeth knowledge without the fear of God ?

Surely, an humble husbandman that serveth God is better than a proud philosopher that neglecting himself laboureth to understand the course of the heavens.

Whoso knoweth himself well, groweth more mean in his own conceit, and delighteth not in the praises of men.

If I understood all things in the world, and were not in charity, what would that help me in the sight of God, who will judge me according to my deeds?

II. Cease from an inordinate desire of knowing, for therein is much distraction and deceit.

The learned are well-pleased to seem so to others, and to be accounted wise.[2]

There be many things, which to know doth little or nothing profit the soul :

And he is very unwise, that is intent upon other things than those that may avail him for his salvation.

Many words do not satisfy the soul ; but a good life comforteth the mind, and a pure conscience giveth great assurance in the sight of God.

III. How much the more thou knowest, and how much the better thou understandest, so much the more grievously shalt thou therefore be judged, unless thy life be also more holy.

Be not therefore extolled in thine own mind for any art or science, but rather let the knowledge given thee, make thee more humble and cautious.

If thou thinkest that thou understandest and knowest much ; know also that there be many things more which thou knowest not.

---

[1] Eccles. i. [13] ; Arist. Met. I. 1.   [2] 1 Cor. viii. [1].

Affect not to be overwise, but rather acknowledge thine own ignorance.[1]

Why wilt thou prefer thyself before others, sith there be many more learned, and more skilful in the Scripture than thou art?

If thou wilt know or learn anything profitably, desire to be unknown, and to be little esteemed.

IV. The highest and most profitable reading, is the true knowledge and consideration of ourselves.

It is great wisdom and perfection to esteem nothing of ourselves, and to think always well and highly of others.

If thou shouldest see another openly sin, or commit some heinous offence, yet oughtest thou not to esteem the better of thyself; for thou knowest not how long thou shalt be able to remain in good estate.

We are all frail,[2] but thou oughtest to esteem none more frail than thyself.

CHAPTER III

OF THE DOCTRINE OF TRUTH

HAPPY is he whom truth by itself doth teach,[3] not by figures and words that pass away; but as it is in itself.

Our own opinion and our own sense do often deceive us, and they discern but little.

What availeth it to cavil and dispute much about dark and hidden things;[4] whereas for being ignorant of them we shall not be so much as reproved at the day of judgment?

It is a great folly to neglect the things that are profitable and necessary, and give our minds to that which is curious and hurtful: we have eyes and see not.[5]

II. And what have we to do with *genus* and *species*, the dry notions of logicians?

---

[1] Rom. xii. [16].   [2] Gen. viii. [21].   [3] Psalm xciv. [12].
[4] Eccles. iii. [9-11].   [5] Psalm cxv. [5].

He to whom the Eternal Word speaketh, is delivered from a world of unnecessary conceptions.

From that one Word are all things, and all speak that one ; and this is the Beginning, which also speaketh unto us.

No man without that Word understandeth or judgeth rightly.

He to whom all things are one, he who reduceth all things to one, and seeth all things in one ; may enjoy a quiet mind, and remain peaceable in God.

O God, who art the truth, make me one with Thee in everlasting charity.

It is tedious to me often to read and hear many things : In Thee is all that I would have and can desire.

Let all doctors hold their peace ; let all creatures be silent in Thy sight ; speak Thou alone unto me.

III. The more a man is united within himself, and becometh inwardly simple and pure, so much the more and higher things doth he understand without labour ; for that he receiveth intellectual light from above.[1]

A pure, sincere, and stable spirit is not distracted, though it be employed in many works ; for that it works all to the honour of God, and inwardly being still and quiet, seeks not itself in any thing it doth.

Who hinders and troubles thee more than the unmortified affections of thine own heart?

A good and godly man disposeth within himself beforehand those things which he is outwardly to act ;

Neither do they draw him according to the desires of an inordinate inclination, but he ordereth them according to the prescript of right reason.

Who hath a greater combat than he that laboureth to overcome himself?

This ought to be our endeavour, to conquer ourselves, and daily to wax stronger, and to make a further growth in holiness.

IV. All perfection in this life hath some imperfection

[1] Matt. xi. [25]; Luke x. [21].

mixed with it; and no knowledge of ours is without some darkness.

An humble knowledge of thyself is a surer way to God than a deep search after learning;

Yet learning is not to be blamed, nor the mere knowledge of any thing whatsoever to be disliked, it being good in itself, and ordained by God; but a good conscience and a virtuous life is always to be preferred before it.

But because many endeavour rather to get knowledge than to live well; therefore they are often deceived, and reap either none, or but little fruit.

V. O, if men bestowed as much labour in the rooting out of vices, and planting of virtues, as they do in moving of questions, neither would there so much hurt be done, nor so great scandal be given in the world, nor so much looseness be practised in Religious Houses.

Truly, at the day. of judgment we shall not be examined what we have read, but what we have done;[1] not how well we have spoken, but how religiously we have lived.

Tell me now, where are all those Doctors and Masters, with whom thou wast well acquainted, whilst they lived and flourished in learning?

Now others possess their livings and perhaps do scarce ever think of them. In their lifetime they seemed something, but now they are not spoken of.

VI. O, how quickly doth the glory of the world pass away![2] O that their life had been answerable to their learning! then had their study and reading been to good purpose.

How many perish by reason of vain learning[3] in this world, who take little care of the serving of God:

And because they rather choose to be great than humble, therefore they become vain in their imaginations.[4]

---

[1] Matt. xxv.   [2] Eccles. ii. [11].   [3] Tit. i. [10].
[4] Rom. i. [21].

He is truly great, that is great in charity.

He is truly great, that is little in himself, and that maketh no account of any height of honour.[1]

He is truly wise, that accounteth all earthly things as dung, that he may gain Christ.[2]

And he is truly learned, that doeth the will of God, and forsaketh his own will.

CHAPTER IV

OF WISDOM AND FORETHOUGHT IN OUR ACTIONS

WE must not give ear to every saying or suggestion,[3] but ought warily and leisurely to ponder things according to the will of God.

But alas ; such is our weakness, that we often rather believe and speak evil of others than good.

Those that are perfect men do not easily give credit to every thing one tells them ; for they know that human frailty is prone to evil,[4] and very subject to fail in words.[5]

II. It is great wisdom not to be rash in thy proceedings,[6] nor to stand stiffly in thine own conceits ;

As also not to believe every thing which thou hearest, nor presently to relate again to others[7] what thou hast heard or dost believe.

Consult with him that is wise and conscientious, and seek to be instructed by a better than thyself, rather than to follow thine own inventions.[8]

A good life maketh a man wise according to God,[9] and giveth him experience in many things.[10]

The more humble a man is in himself, and the more subject unto God ; so much the more prudent shall he be in all his affairs, and enjoy greater peace and quiet of heart.

[1] Matt. xviii. [4] ; xxiii. [11].   [2] Phil. iii. [8].
[3] 1 John iv. [1].   [4] Gen. viii. [21].   [5] James iii. [2].
[6] Prov. xix. [2].   [7] Prov. xvii. [9].   [8] Prov. xii. [15].
[9] Prov. xv. [33].   [10] Eccles. i. [16].

CHAPTER V

OF THE READING OF HOLY SCRIPTURES

TRUTH, not eloquence, is to be sought for in Holy Scripture.

Each part of the Scripture is to be read with the same Spirit wherewith it was written.[1]

We should rather search after our spiritual profit in the Scriptures, than subtilty of speech.

We ought to read plain and devout books as willingly as high and profound.

Let not the authority of the writer offend thee, whether he be of great or small learning ; but let the love of pure truth draw thee to read.[2]

Search not who spoke this or that, but mark what is spoken.

II. Men pass away, but the truth of the Lord remaineth for ever.[3] God speaks unto us sundry ways without respect of persons.[4]

Our own curiosity often hindereth us in reading of the Scriptures, when as we will examine and discuss that which we should rather pass over without more ado.

If thou desire to reap profit, read with humility, simplicity, and faithfulness ; nor ever desire the estimation of learning.

Enquire willingly, and hear with silence the words of holy men ; dislike not the parables of the Elders, for they are not recounted without cause.[5]

[1] Rom. xv. [4].   [2] 1 Cor. ii. [4].
[3] Psalm cxvii. [2] ; Luke xxi. [33].
[4] Rom. ii. [11]: x. [12] ; Col. iii. [11].
[5] Prov. i. [6] ; Eccles. xii. [9].

CHAPTER VI

OF INORDINATE AFFECTIONS

Whensoever a man desireth any thing inordinately, he is presently disquieted in himself.

The proud and covetous can never rest. The poor and humble in spirit live together in all peace.

The man that is not yet perfectly dead to himself, is quickly tempted and overcome in small and trifling things.

The weak in spirit, and he that is yet in a manner carnal and prone to sensible things, can hardly withdraw himself altogether from earthly desires :

And therefore he is often afflicted, when he goeth about to withdraw himself from them ; and easily falleth into indignation, when any opposition is made against him.

II. And if he hath followed therein his appetite, he is presently disquieted with remorse of conscience ; for that he yielded to his passion, which profiteth him nothing to the obtaining of the peace he sought for.

True quietness of heart therefore is gotten by resist· ing our passions, not by obeying them.

There is then no peace in the heart of a carnal man, nor in him that is addicted to outward things, but in the spiritual and fervent man.

CHAPTER VII

OF FLYING VAIN HOPE AND PRIDE

He is vain that putteth his trust in man,[1] or creatures.

Be not ashamed to serve others for the love of Jesus Christ ; nor to be esteemed poor in this world.

[1] Jer. xvii. [5].

Presume not upon thyself, but place thy hope in God.[1]

Do what lieth in thy power and God will assist thy good affection.

Trust not in thine own knowledge,[2] nor in the subtilty of any living creature ; but rather in the grace of God, who helpeth the humble, and humbleth those that are proud.

II. Glory not in wealth if thou have it, nor in friends because potent ; but in God who giveth all things, and above all desireth to give thee Himself.

Extol not thyself for the height of thy stature or beauty of thy person, which may be disfigured and destroyed with a little sickness.

Take not pleasure in thy natural gifts, or wit, lest thereby thou displease God, to whom appertaineth all the good whatsoever thou hast by nature.

III. Esteem not thyself better than others,[3] lest perhaps in the sight of God, who knoweth what is in man, thou be accounted worse than they.

Be not proud of well-doing ;[4] for the judgment of God is far different from the judgment of men, and that often offendeth Him which pleaseth them.

If there be any good in thee, believe that there is much more in others, that so thou mayest conserve humility within thee.

It is no prejudice unto thee to debase thyself under all men ; but it is very prejudicial to thee to prefer thyself before any one man.

The humble enjoy continual peace, but in the heart of the proud is envy, and frequent indignation.

[1] Psalm xxxi. [1].   [2] Jer. ix. [23].   [3] Exod. iii. [11].
[4] Job ix. [20].

CHAPTER VIII

THAT TOO MUCH FAMILIARITY IS TO BE SHUNNED

LAY not thy heart open to every one; but treat of thy affairs with the wise, and such as fear God.[1]

Converse not much with young people and strangers.[2]

Flatter not the rich: neither do thou appear willingly before great personages.

Keep company with the humble and plain ones, with the devout and virtuous; and confer with them of those things that may edify. Be not familiar with any woman; but in general commend all good women to God.

Desire to be familiar with God alone and His Angels, and avoid the acquaintance of men.

II. We must have charity towards all, but familiarity with all is not expedient.

Sometimes it falleth out, that a person unknown to us, is much esteemed of, from the good report given him by others; whose presence notwithstanding is not grateful to the eyes of the beholders.

We think sometimes to please others by our company, and we rather distaste them with those bad qualities which they discover in us.

CHAPTER IX

OF OBEDIENCE AND SUBJECTION

IT is a great matter to live in obedience, to be under a superior, and not to be at our own disposing.

It is much safer to obey, than to govern.

Many live under obedience, rather for necessity than

---

[1] Eccles. viii. [12].   [2] Prov. v. [10].

for charity ; such are discontented, and do easily repine.
Neither can they attain to freedom of mind, unless
they willingly and heartily put themselves under
obedience for the love of God.

Go whither thou wilt, thou shalt find no rest, but in
humble subjection under the government of a superior.
The imagination and change of places have deceived
many.

II. True it is, that every one willingly doth that
which agreeth with his own sense, and is apt to affect
those most that are of his own mind ;

But if God be amongst us, we must sometimes
cease, to adhere to our own opinion for the sake of
peace.

Who is so wise that he can fully know all things ;

Be not therefore too confident in thine own opinion ;
but be willing to hear the judgment of others.

If that which thou thinkest be not amiss, and yet
thou partest with it for God, and followest the opinion
of another, it shall be better for thee.

III. I have often heard, that it is safer to hear and
take counsel, than to give it.

It may also fall out, that each one's opinion may be
good ; but to refuse to yield to others when reason or a
special cause requireth it, is a sign of pride and stiff-
ness.

CHAPTER X

OF AVOIDING SUPERFLUITY IN WORDS

Fly the tumultuousness of the world as much as
thou canst ; [1] for the talk of worldly affairs is a great
hindrance, although they be discoursed of with sincere
intention ;

For we are quickly defiled, and enthralled with
vanity.

[1] Matt. iv. [1] ; xiv. [23] ; John vi. [15].

Oftentimes I could wish that I had held my peace when I have spoken ; and that I had not been in company.

Why do we so willingly speak and talk one with another, when notwithstanding we seldom return to silence without hurt of conscience ?[1]

The cause why we so willingly talk, is for that by discoursing one with another, we seek to receive comfort one of another, and desire to ease our mind over-wearied with sundry thoughts :

And we very willingly talk and think of those things which we most love or desire ; or of those which we feel most contrary unto us.

II. But alas, oftentimes in vain, and to no end ; for this outward comfort is the cause of no small loss of inward and divine consolation.

Therefore we must watch and pray, lest our time pass away idly.

If it be lawful and expedient for thee to speak, speak those things that may edify.

An evil custom and neglect of our own good doth give too much liberty to inconsiderate speech.

Yet religious discourses of spiritual things do greatly further our spiritual growth, especially when persons of one mind and spirit be gathered together in God.[2]

CHAPTER XI

OF THE OBTAINING OF PEACE, AND ZEALOUS DESIRE OF PROGRESS IN GRACE

WE might enjoy much peace, if we would not busy ourselves with the words and deeds of other men, with things which appertain nothing to our charge.

How can he abide long in peace, who thrusts himself into the cares of others, who seeks occasions abroad,

[1] Matt. vii. [1]; Rom. ii. [1].
[2] Acts i. [14] ; Rom. xv. [5, 6].

who little or seldom recollects himself within his own breast?

Blessed are the single-hearted ; for they shall enjoy much peace.

II. What is the reason, why some of the Saints were so perfect and contemplative?

Because they laboured to mortify themselves wholly to all earthly desires ; and therefore they could with their whole heart fix themselves upon God, and be free for holy retirement.

We are too much led by our passions, and too solicitous for transitory things.

We also seldom overcome any one vice perfectly, and are not inflamed with a fervent desire to grow better every day ; and therefore we remain cold and lukewarm.

III. If we were perfectly dead unto ourselves, and not entangled within our own breasts ; then should we be able to taste divine things, and to have some experience of heavenly contemplation.

The greatest and indeed the whole impediment is for that we are not disentangled from our passions and lusts, neither do we endeavour to enter into that path of perfection, which the Saints have walked before us ; and when any small adversity befalleth us, we are too quickly dejected, and turn ourselves to human comforts.

IV. If we would endeavour like men of courage to stand in the battle, surely we should feel the favourable assistance of God from Heaven.

For He who giveth us occasion to fight, to the end we may get the victory, is ready to succour those that fight manfully, and do trust in His grace.

If we esteem our progress in religious life to consist only in some exterior observances, our devotion will quickly be at an end.

But let us lay the axe to the root, that being freed from passions, we may find rest to our souls.

V. If every year we would root out one vice, we should sooner become perfect men.

But now oftentimes we perceive it goes contrary, and that we were better and purer at the beginning of our conversion, than after many years of our profession.

Our fervour and profiting should increase daily : but now it is accounted a great matter, if a man can retain but some part of his first zeal.

If we would but a little force ourselves at the beginning, then should we be able to perform all things afterwards with ease and delight.

VI. It is a hard matter to leave off that to which we are accustomed, but it is harder to go against our own wills.

But if thou dost not overcome little and easy things, how wilt thou overcome harder things?

Resist thy inclination in the very beginning, and unlearn evil customs, lest perhaps by little and little they draw thee to greater difficulty.

O if thou didst but consider how much inward peace unto thyself, and joy unto others, thou shouldst procure by demeaning thyself well, I suppose thou wouldest be more careful of thy spiritual progress.

CHAPTER XII

OF THE PROFIT OF ADVERSITY

It is good that we have sometimes some troubles and crosses ; for they often make a man enter into himself, and consider that he is here in banishment, and ought not to place his trust in any worldly thing.

It is good that we be sometimes contradicted, and that there be an evil or a lessening conceit had of us ; and this, although we do and intend well.

These things help often to the attaining of humility, and defend us from vain glory : for then we chiefly seek God for our inward witness, when outwardly we be contemned by men, and when there is no credit given unto us.

II. And therefore a man should settle himself so fully in God, that he need not to seek many comforts of men.

When a good man is afflicted, tempted, or troubled with evil thoughts; then he understandeth better the great need he hath of God, without whom he perceiveth he can do nothing that is good.

Then also he sorroweth, lamenteth, and prayeth, by reason of the miseries he suffereth.

Then he is weary of living longer, and wisheth that death would come, that he might be dissolved and be with Christ.

Then also he well perceiveth, that perfect security and full peace cannot be had in this world.

CHAPTER XIII

OF RESISTING TEMPTATION

So long as we live in this world we cannot be without tribulation and temptation.

According as it is written in Job, 'The life of man upon earth is a life of temptation.[1]

Every one therefore ought to be careful about his temptations, and to watch in prayer, lest the devil find an advantage to deceive him; who never sleepeth, but goeth about seeking whom he may devour.

No man is so perfect and holy, but he hath sometimes temptations; and altogether without them we cannot be.

II. Nevertheless temptations are often very profitable to us, though they be troublesome and grievous; for in them a man is humbled, purified, and instructed.

All the Saints passed through many tribulations and temptations, and profited thereby.

[1] Job vii. 1.

And they that could not bear temptations, became reprobate, and fell away.

There is no order so holy, nor place so secret, where there be not temptations, or adversities.

III. There is no man that is altogether free from temptations whilst he liveth on earth : for in ourselves is the root thereof, being born with inclination to evil.

When one temptation or tribulation goeth away, another cometh ; and we shall ever have something to suffer, because we are fallen from the state of our felicity.

Many seek to fly temptations, and do fall more grievously into them.

By flight alone we cannot overcome, but by patience and true humility we become stronger than all our enemies.

IV. He that only avoideth them outwardly, and doth not pluck them up by the roots, shall profit little ; yea temptations will the sooner return unto him, and he shall feel himself in a worse case than before.

By little and little, and by patience with long-suffering, through God's help, thou shalt more easily overcome, than with violence and thine own importunity.

Often take counsel in temptations, and deal not roughly with him that is tempted ; but give him comfort, as thou wouldest wish to be done to thyself.

V. The beginning of all evil temptations is inconstancy of mind, and small confidence in God.

For as a ship without a helm is tossed to and fro with the waves ; so the man who is remiss, and apt to leave his purpose, is many ways tempted.

Fire trieth iron, and temptation a just man.

We know not oftentimes what we are able to do, but temptations do shew us what we are.

Yet we must be watchful, especially in the beginning of the temptation ; for the enemy is then more easily overcome, if he be not suffered to enter the door of our hearts, but be resisted without the gate at his first knock.

Wherefore one said, 'Withstand the beginnings, for an after remedy comes often too late.'[1]

For first there cometh to the mind a bare thought of evil, then a strong imagination thereof, afterwards delight, and an evil motion, and then consent.

And so by little and little our wicked enemy getteth complete entrance, whilst he is not resisted in the beginning.

And the longer a man is negligent in resisting, so much the weaker does he become daily in himself, and the enemy stronger against him.

VI. Some suffer great temptations in the beginning of their conversion ; others in the latter end.

Others again are much troubled almost through the whole time of their life.

Some are but easily tempted, according to the wisdom and equity of the Divine appointment, which weigheth the states and deserts of men, and ordaineth all things for the welfare of His own chosen ones.

VII. We ought not therefore to despair when we are tempted, but so much the more fervently to pray unto God, that He will vouchsafe to help us in all tribulations ; who surely, according to the words of St. Paul, will give with the temptation such issue, that we may be able to bear it.[2]

Let us therefore humble our souls under the hand of God in all temptations and tribulations, for He will save and exalt the humble spirit.

VIII. In temptations and afflictions, a man is proved how much he hath profited ; and his reward is thereby the greater, and his graces do more eminently shine forth.

Neither is it any such great thing if a man be devout and fervent, when he feeleth no affliction ; but if in time of adversity he bear himself patiently, there is hope then of great proficiency in grace.

Some are kept from great temptations, and in small ones which do daily occur are often overcome ; to the

---

[1] Ovid. Lib. xii. de Remed. Am.   [2] [1 Cor. x. 13.]

end that being humbled, they may never presume on
themselves in great matters, who are baffled in so small
things.

CHAPTER XIV

OF AVOIDING RASH JUDGMENT

TURN thine eyes unto thyself, and beware thou judge
not the deeds of other men.[1]   In judging of others a
man laboureth in vain, often erreth, and easily sinneth;[2]
but in judging and discussing of himself, he always
laboureth fruitfully.

We often judge of things according as we fancy them;
for private affection bereaves us easily of true judgment.

If God were always the pure intention of our desire,
we should not be so easily troubled, through the repug-
nance of our carnal mind.

II. But oftentimes something lurketh within, or else
occurreth from without, which draweth us after it.

Many secretly seek themselves in what they do, and
know it not.

They seem also to live in good peace of mind, when
things are done according to their will and opinion;
but if things happen otherwise than they desire, they are
straightway moved and much vexed.

The diversities of judgments and opinions, cause
oftentimes dissensions between friends and countrymen,
between religious and devout persons.[3]

III. An old custom is hardly broken,[4] and no man is
willing to be led farther than himself can see.

If thou dost more rely upon thine own reason or
industry, than upon that power which brings thee
under the obedience of JESUS Christ, it will be long
before thou become illuminated; for God will have us

---

[1] Matt. vii. [1]; Rom. xv. [1].   [2] Eccles. iii. [16].
[3] Matt. xii. [25]; Luke xii. [51].   [4] Jer. xiii. [23].

perfectly subject unto Him, that, being inflamed with His love, we may transcend the narrow limits of human reason.

CHAPTER XV

OF WORKS DONE IN CHARITY

For no worldly thing, nor for the love of any man, is any evil to be done ;[1] but yet, for the profit of one that standeth in need, a good work is sometimes to be intermitted without any scruple, or changed also for a better.

For by doing this, a good work is not lost, but changed into a better.

Without charity the exterior work profiteth nothing ;[2] but whatsoever is done of charity, be it never so little and contemptible in the sight of the world, it becomes wholly fruitful.

For God weigheth more with how much love a man worketh, than how much he doeth. He doeth much that loveth much.

II. He doeth much, that doeth a thing well.

He doeth well that rather serveth the community, than his own will.[3]

Oftentimes it seemeth to be charity, and it is rather carnality; because natural inclination, self-will, hope of reward, and desire of our own interest, will seldom be away.

III. He that hath true and perfect charity, seeketh himself in nothing :[4] but only desireth in all things that the glory of God should be exalted.

He also envieth none; because he affecteth no private good; neither will he rejoice in himself; but wisheth above all things to be made happy in the enjoyment of God.[5]

[1] Matt. xviii. [8].   [2] 1 Cor. xiii. [3]; Luke vii. [47].
[3] Phil. ii. [17].   [4] Phil. ii. [21]; 1 Cor. xiii. [5].
        [5] Psalm xvii. [15]; xxiv. [6].

He attributeth nothing that is good to any man, but wholly referreth it unto God, from whom as from the fountain all things proceed; in whom finally all the saints do rest as in their highest fruition.

O he that hath but one spark of true charity, would certainly discern that all earthly things be full of vanity.

✗   CHAPTER XVI

OF BEARING WITH THE DEFECTS OF OTHERS

THOSE things that a man cannot amend in himself or in others, he ought to suffer patiently, until God order things otherwise.

Think that perhaps it is better so for thy trial and patience, without which all our good deeds are not much to be esteemed.

Thou oughtest to pray notwithstanding when thou hast such impediments, that God would vouchsafe to help thee, and that thou mayest bear them kindly.[1]

II. If one that is once or twice warned will not give over, contend not with him: but commit all to God, that His will may be fulfilled,[2] and His name honoured in all His servants, who well knoweth how to turn evil into good.

Endeavour to be patient in bearing with the defects and infirmities of others, of what sort soever they be; for that thyself also hast many failings which must be borne with by others.[3]

If thou canst not make thyself such an one as thou wouldest, how canst thou expect to have another in all things to thy liking?

We would willingly have others perfect, and yet we amend not our own faults.

---

[1] Matt. vi. [13]: Luke xi. [4].   [2] Matt. vi. [10].
[3] 1 Thess. v. [14]; Gal. vi. [1].

III. We will have others severely corrected, and will not be corrected ourselves.

The large liberty of others displeaseth us ; and yet we will not have our own desires denied us.

We will have others kept under by strict laws ; but in no sort will ourselves be restrained.

And thus it appeareth, how seldom we weigh our neighbour in the same balance with ourselves.

If all men were perfect, what should we have to suffer of our neighbour for God ?

IV. But now God hath thus ordered it, that we may learn to bear one another's burdens ;[1] for no man is without fault ; no man but hath his burden ; no man sufficient of himself ; no man wise enough of himself ; but we ought to bear with one another, comfort one another, help, instruct, and admonish one another.[2]

Occasions of adversity best discover how great virtue or strength each one hath.

For occasions do not make a man frail, but they shew what he is.

CHAPTER XVII

OF A RETIRED LIFE

Thou must learn to break thy own will in many things if thou wilt have peace and concord with others.[3]

It is no small matter to dwell in a religious community, or congregation, to converse therein without complaint, and to persevere therein faithfully unto death.[4]

Blessed is he that hath there lived well, and ended happily.

If thou wilt persevere in grace as thou oughtest, and grow therein, esteem thyself as a banished man, and a pilgrim upon earth.[5]

[1] Gal. vi. [2].   [2] 1 Thess. v. [14] ; 1 Cor. xii. [25].
[3] Gal. vi. [1].   [4] Luke xvi. [10].   [5] 1 Pet. ii. [11].

Thou must be contented for Christ's sake to be esteemed as a fool in this world, if thou desire to lead a religious life.

II. The wearing of a religious habit, and shaving of the crown, do little profit; but change of manners, and perfect mortification of passions, make a true religious man.

He that seeketh anything else but merely God, and the salvation of his soul, shall find nothing but tribulation and sorrow.[1]

Neither can he remain long in peace, that laboureth not to be the least, and subject unto all.

III. Thou camest to serve, not to rule.[2] Know that thou wast called to suffer and to labour, not to be idle, or to spend thy time in talk.

Here therefore men are proved as gold in the furnace.

Here no man can stand, unless he humble himself with his whole heart for the love of God.

CHAPTER XVIII

OF THE EXAMPLES OF THE HOLY FATHERS

CONSIDER the lively examples of the holy Fathers, in whom true perfection and religion shined;[3] and thou shalt see how little it is, and almost nothing, which we do now in these days.

Alas! what is our life, if it be compared to them!

The Saints and friends of Christ served the Lord in hunger and thirst, in cold and nakedness, in labour and weariness, in watchings and fastings, in prayer and holy meditations, in many persecutions and reproaches.

II. O how many and grievous tribulations suffered

---

[1] Eccles. i. [17, 18] ; Ecclus. i. [18].   [2] Matt. xx. [26].
[3] Heb. xi.

the Apostles, Martyrs, Confessors, Virgins, and all the rest that endeavoured to follow the steps of Christ !

For they hated their lives in this world, that they might keep them unto life eternal.[1]

O how strict and self-renouncing a life, led those holy Fathers in the wilderness ![2] How long and grievous temptations suffered they ! How often were they assaulted by the enemy ! What frequent and fervent prayers offered they to God ! What rigorous abstinences did they use ! How great zeal and care had they of their spiritual proficiency ! How strong a combat had they for the overcoming of their lusts ! How pure and upright intentions kept they towards God !

In the day they laboured, and in the night they attended to continual prayer : although when they laboured also, they ceased not from mental prayer.

III. They spent all their time with profit ; every hour seemed short for the service of God.

And by reason of the great sweetness they felt in contemplation, they forgot the necessity of corporal refreshments.

They renounced all riches, dignities, honours, friends, and kinsfolk ;[3] they desired to have nothing which appertained to the world ; they scarce took things necessary for the sustenance of life ; they grieved to serve their bodies even in necessity.

Therefore they were poor in earthly things, but very rich in grace and virtues.

Outwardly they were destitute, but inwardly they were refreshed with grace and divine consolation.

IV. They were strangers to the world, but near and familiar friends to God.[4]

They seemed to themselves as nothing, and to this present world despicable ; but they were precious and beloved in the eyes of God.

[1] John xii. [25].   [2] Matt. vii. [14].
[3] Matt. xix. [29].   [4] James iv. [4].

They were grounded in true humility, lived in simple obedience, walked in love and patience : and therefore they profited daily in the Spirit, and obtained great grace in God's sight.

They were given for an example to all religious men ; and they should more provoke us to endeavour after spiritual proficiencies, than the number of the lukewarm livers should prevail to make us remiss.

V. O how great was the fervour of all religious persons in the beginning of their holy institution !

How great was their devotion to prayer ! What ambition to excel others in virtue ! How exact discipline then flourished ! How great reverence and obedience, under the rule of their superiors, observed they in all things !

Their footsteps yet remaining, do testify that they were indeed holy and perfect men ; who fighting so valiantly trod the world under their feet.

Now, he is greatly accounted of, who is not a transgressor, and who can with patience endure that which he hath undertaken.

VI. O the lukewarmness and negligence of our times ! that we so quickly decline from the ancient fervour, and are come to that pass, that very sloth and lukewarmness of spirit maketh our own life tedious unto us.

Would to God the desire to grow in virtues did not wholly sleep in thee, who hast often seen the many examples of devout and religious persons !

CHAPTER XIX

OF THE EXERCISES OF A GOOD RELIGIOUS PERSON

THE life of a good religious person ought to be adorned with all virtues ;[1] that he may inwardly be such as outwardly he seemeth to men.

[1] Matt. v. [48].

And with reason there ought to be much more within, than is perceived without. For God beholdeth us;[1] whom we are bound most highly to reverence wheresoever we are, and to walk in purity[2] like Angels in His sight.

Daily ought we to renew our purposes, and to stir up ourselves to greater fervour, as though this were the first day of our conversion; and to say,

'Help me, my God! in this my good purpose, and in Thy holy service; and grant that I may now this day begin perfectly; for that which I have done hitherto is as nothing.'

II. According to our purpose shall be the success of our spiritual profiting; and much diligence is necessary to him that will profit much.

And if he that firmly purposeth often faileth, what shall he do that seldom purposeth any thing, or with little resolvedness;

It may fall out sundry ways that we leave off our purpose; yet the light omission of our spiritual exercises seldom passes without some loss to our souls.

The purpose of just men depends not upon their own wisdom, but upon God's grace; on whom they always rely for whatsoever they take in hand.

For man purposes, but God disposes;[3] neither is the way of man in himself.

III. If an accustomed exercise be sometimes omitted, either for some act of piety, or profit to my brother; it may easily afterwards be recovered again.

But if out of a slothful mind, or out of carelessness, we lightly forsake the same, it is a great offence against God, and will be found to be prejudicial to ourselves. Let us do the best we can, we shall still too easily fail in many things.[4]

Yet must we always purpose some certain course, and especially against those failings which do most of all molest us.

---

[1] Psalm xxxiii. [13]; Heb. iv. [12, 13].   [2] Psalm xv. [2].
[3] Prov. xvi. [9].   [4] Eccles. vii. [20].

We must diligently search into, and set in order both the outward and the inward man, because both of them are of importance to our progress in godliness.

IV. If thou canst not continually recollect thyself, yet do it sometimes, at the least once a day, namely, in the morning or at night.

In the morning fix thy good purpose; and at night examine thyself what thou hast done, how thou hast behaved thyself in word, deed, and thought;[1] for in these perhaps thou hast oftentimes offended both God and thy neighbour.

Gird up thy loins like a man against the vile assaults of the devil; bridle thy riotous appetite, and thou shalt be the better able to keep under all the unruly motions of the flesh.

Never be entirely idle; but either be reading, or writing, or praying, or meditating, or endeavouring something for the public good.

As for bodily exercises they must be used with discretion, neither are they to be practised of all men alike.

V. Those devotions which belong not to the community are not to be exposed to public view; for things private are practised more safely at home.

Nevertheless thou must beware thou neglect not those which are common, being more ready for what is private. But having fully and faithfully accomplished all which thou art bound and enjoined to do, if thou hast any spare time, betake thee to thyself, as thy devotion shall desire.

All cannot use one kind of spiritual exercise, but one is more useful for this person, another for that.

According to the seasonableness of times also, divers exercises are fitting; some suit better with us on working days, other on holy days.

In the time of temptation, we have need of some, and of others in time of peace and quietness.

Some we mind when we are pensive, and other some when we rejoice in the Lord.

[1] Deut. iv.

VI. About the time of the chief festivals, good exercises are to be renewed, and the prayers of holy men more fervently to be implored.

From festival to festival we should make some good purpose, as though we were then to depart out of this world, and to come to the everlasting feast.

Therefore ought we carefully to prepare ourselves at holy times, and to live more devoutly, and to keep more exactly all things that we are to observe, as though we were shortly at God's hands to receive the reward of our labours.

VII. But if it be deferred, let us think with ourselves that we are not sufficiently prepared, and unworthy yet of so great glory which shall be revealed in us[1] in due time ; and let us endeavour to prepare ourselves better for our departure.

' Blessed is that servant (saith the Evangelist St. Luke) whom his Lord when He cometh shall find watching : Verily, I say unto you, He shall make him ruler over all His goods.'[2]

CHAPTER XX

OF THE LOVE OF SOLITUDE AND SILENCE

SEEK a convenient time[3] to retire into thyself, and meditate often upon God's lovingkindness.

Meddle not with curiosities ; but read such things as may rather yield compunction to thy heart, than occupation to thy head.

If thou wilt withdraw thyself from speaking vainly, and from gadding idly, as also from hearkening after novelties and rumours, thou shalt find leisure enough and suitable for meditation on good things.

The greatest Saints avoided the society of men,[4]

[1] Rom. viii. [18].
[2] Luke xii. [43, 44] ; Matt. xxiv. [46, 47].
[3] Eccles. iii. [1].   [4] Heb. xi. [38].

when they could conveniently, and did rather choose to live to God, in secret.

II. One said, ' As oft as I have been among men, I returned home less a man than I was before.' [1]

And this we find true, when we talk long together. It is easier not to speak a word at all, than not to speak more words than we should.

It is easier for a man to keep at home, than to keep himself well when he is abroad.

He therefore that intends to attain to the more inward and spiritual things of religion, must with JESUS depart from the multitude and press of people. [2]

No man doth safely appear abroad, but he who gladly can abide at home, out of sight.

No man speaks securely, but he that holds his peace willingly. [3]

No man ruleth safely, but he that is willingly ruled.

No man securely doth command but he that hath learned readily to obey.

III. No man rejoiceth securely, unless he hath within him the testimony of a good conscience.

And yet always the security of the Saints was full of the fear of God.

Neither were they the less anxious and humble in themselves, for that they shined outwardly with grace and great virtues.

But the security of bad men ariseth from pride and presumption, and in the end it deceiveth them.

Although thou seem to be a good religious man, or a devout solitary, yet never promise thyself security in this life.

IV. Oftentimes those who have been in the greatest esteem and account amongst men, have fallen into the greatest danger, by overmuch self-confidence.

Wherefore to many it is more profitable not to be altogether free from temptations, but to be often assaulted, lest they should be too secure, and so perhaps

[1] Seneca, Ep. vii.   [2] Matt. v. [1].
[3] Eccles. ii. [7].

be puffed up with pride ; or else too freely give themselves to worldly comforts.

O how good a conscience should he keep, that would never seek after transitory joy, nor ever entangle himself with the things of this world !

O how great peace and quietness should he possess, that would cut off all vain anxiety, and think only upon divine things, and such as are profitable for his soul, and would place all his confidence in God.

V. No man is worthy of heavenly comfort, unless he have diligently exercised himself in holy compunction.

If thou desirest true contrition of heart, enter into thy secret chamber, and shut out the tumults of the world, as it is written, 'In your chambers be ye grieved.'[1]   In thy chamber thou shalt find what abroad thou shalt too often lose.

The more thou visitest thy chamber, the more thou wilt like it ; the less thou comest thereunto, the more thou wilt loath it.   If in the beginning of thy conversion thou art content to remain in it, and keep to it well, it will afterwards be to thee a dear friend, and a most pleasant comfort.

VI. In silence and in stillness a religious soul advantageth herself, and learneth the mysteries of Holy Scripture.

There she findeth rivers of tears, wherein she may every night[2] wash and cleanse herself ; that she may be so much the more familiar with her Creator, by how much the farther off she liveth from all worldly disquiet.

Whoso therefore withdraweth himself from his acquaintance and friends, God will draw near unto him with His holy Angels.

It is better for a man to live privately, and to take care of himself, than to neglect his soul, though he could work wonders in the world.

It is commendable in a religious person, seldom to go abroad, to be unwilling to see or to be seen.

VII. Why art thou desirous to see that which it is

[1] Psalm iv. [4. Latin Version].   [2] Psalm vi. [6].

unlawful for thee to have? The world passeth away and the lust thereof.

Our sensual desires draw us to rove abroad; but when the time is past, what carriest thou home with thee but a burdened conscience and distracted heart?

A merry going out bringeth often a mournful return home; and a joyful evening makes often a sad morning.[1]

So all carnal joy enters gently, but in the end it bites and stings to death.

What canst thou see elsewhere, which thou canst not see here?[2] Behold the heaven and the earth and all the elements; for of these are all things created.

VIII. What canst thou see any where that can long continue under the sun?

Thou thinkest perchance to satisfy thyself, but thou canst never attain it.

Shouldest thou see all things present before thine eyes, what were it but a vain sight?[3]

Lift up thine eyes[4] to God in the highest, and pray Him to pardon thy sins and negligences.

Leave vain things to the vain; but be thou intent upon those things which God hath commanded thee.

Shut thy door upon thee,[5] and call unto thee JESUS, thy Beloved.

Stay with Him in thy closet; for thou shalt not find so great peace any where else.

If thou hadst not gone abroad and hearkened to idle rumours, thou wouldest the better have preserved a happy peace of mind. But since thou delightest sometimes to hear novelties, it is but fit thou suffer for it some disquietude of heart.

[1] Prov. xiv. [13].   [2] Eccles. i. [10].
[3] Eccles. iii. [11].   [4] Psalm cxxi. [1].
[5] Matt. vi. [6].

CHAPTER XXI

OF COMPUNCTION OF HEART

IF thou wilt make any progress in godliness, keep thyself in the fear of God,[1] and affect not too much liberty. Restrain all thy senses under discipline, and give not thyself over to foolish mirth.

Give thyself to compunction of heart, and thou shalt gain much devotion thereby.

Compunction layeth open much good, which dissoluteness is wont quickly to destroy.

It is a wonder that any man can ever perfectly rejoice in this life, if he duly consider, and thoroughly weigh his state of banishment, and the many perils wherewith his soul is environed.

II. Through levity of heart, and small care for our failings, we become insensible of the real sorrows of our souls ; and so oftentimes we vainly laugh, when we have just cause to weep.

There is no true liberty nor right joy but in the fear of God accompanied with a good conscience.

Happy is he, who can cast off all distracting impediments, and bring himself to the one single purpose of holy compunction.

Happy is he, who can abandon all that may defile his conscience or burden it.

Resist manfully ; one custom overcometh another.

If thou canst let others alone in their matters, they likewise shall not hinder thee in thine.

III. Busy not thyself in matters which appertain to others ; neither do thou entangle thyself with the affairs of thy betters.

Still have an eye to thyself first, and be sure more especially to admonish thyself before all thy beloved friends.

If thou hast not the favour of men, be not grieved at it ;[2] but take this to heart, that thou dost not behave

---

[1] Prov. xix. [23].   [2] Gal. i. [10].

thyself so warily and circumspectly as it becometh the servant of God, and a devout religious man.

It is better oftentimes and safer that a man should not have many consolations in this life,[1] especially such as are according to the flesh.

But that we have not divine consolations at all, or do very seldom taste them, the fault is ours, because we seek not after compunction of heart, nor do altogether forsake the vain and outward comforts of this world.

IV. Know that thou art unworthy of divine consolation, and that thou hast rather deserved much tribulation.

When a man hath perfect contrition, then is the whole world grievous and bitter unto him.[2]

A good man findeth always sufficient cause for mourning and weeping.

For whether he consider his own or his neighbour's estate, he knoweth that none liveth here without tribulation.

And the more narrowly a man looks into himself, so much the more he sorroweth.

Our sins and wickednesses wherein we lie so enwrapt, that we can seldom apply ourselves to Heavenly contemplations, do minister unto us matter of just sorrow and inward compunction.

V. Didst thou oftener think of thy death,[3] than of thy living long, there is no question but thou wouldst be more zealous to amend.

If also thou didst but consider within thyself the infernal pains in the other world,[4] I believe thou wouldst willingly undergo any labour or sorrow in this world, and not be afraid of the greatest austerity.

But because these things enter not to the heart, and we still love those things only that delight us, therefore it is we remain cold and very dull in religion.

---

[1] Psalm lxxvi. [5].

[2] Judges ii. [4]; xx. [26]. 2 Kings xiii. [perhaps 2 Sam. xii. 17].

[3] Eccles. vii. [1, 2]. [4] Matt. xxv. [41].

D

VI. It is often our want of spirit which maketh our miserable body so easily complain.

Pray therefore unto the Lord with all humility, that He will vouchsafe to give thee the spirit of compunction.   And say with the Prophet, 'Feed me, O Lord, with the bread of tears, and give me plenteousness of tears to drink.'[1]

CHAPTER XXII

OF THE CONSIDERATION OF HUMAN MISERY

MISERABLE thou art, wheresoever thou be, or whithersoever thou turnest, unless thou turn thyself unto God.

Why art thou troubled when things succeed not as thou wouldest or desirest?   For who is he that hath all things according to his mind?[2] neither I nor thou, nor any man upon earth.

There is none in this world, even though he be King or Bishop, without some tribulation or perplexity.

Who is then in the best case? even he who is able to suffer something for God.

II. Many weak and infirm persons say, Behold! what a happy life such an one leads:[3] how wealthy, how great he is, in what power and dignity!

But lift up thine eyes to the riches of Heaven, and thou shalt see that all the goods of this life are nothing to be accounted of.   They are very uncertain, and rather burdensome than otherwise, because they are never possessed without anxiety and fear.

Man's happiness consisteth not in having abundance of temporal goods,[4] but a moderate portion is sufficient for him.

Truly it is misery even to live upon the earth.[5]

[1] Psalm lxxx. [5].   [2] Eccles. vi. [2].
[3] Luke xii. [19].   [4] Prov. xix. [1].
           [5] Job xiv. [1] ; Eccles. ii. [17].

The more spiritual a man desires to be, the more bitter does this present life become to him ; because he sees more clearly and perceives more sensibly the defects of human corruption.

For to eat and to drink, to sleep and to watch, to labour and to rest, and to be subject to other necessities of nature, is doubtless a great misery and affliction to a religious man, who would gladly be set loose, and free from all sin.

III. For the inward man is much weighed down with these outward and corporal necessities whilst we live in this world.

Therefore the Prophet prayeth with great devotion to be enabled to be free from them, saying, ' Bring me, O Lord, out of my necessities.' [1]

But woe be to them that know not their own misery; and a greater woe to them that love this miserable and corruptible life ! [2]

For some there be who so much doat upon it, that although by labour or by begging they can scarce get mere necessaries, yet if they might be able to live here always, they would care nothing at all for the Kingdom of God.

IV. O how senseless are these men and unbelieving in heart, who lie so deeply sunk in the earth, that they can relish nothing but carnal things ! [3]

But miserable as they are, they shall in the end feel to their cost how vile and how nothing that was which they loved.

Whereas the Saints of God and all the devout friends of Christ regarded not those things which pleased the flesh, nor those which flourished in this life, but longed after the everlasting riches [4] with their whole hope and earnest intention.

Their whole desire was carried upward to things durable and invisible, that the desire of things visible might not draw them to things below.

[1] Psalm xxv. [17].   [2] Rom. viii. [22].
[3] Rom. viii. [5].   [4] 1 Pet. i. [4]; Heb. xi. [26].

V. O my brother, lose not thy confidence of making progress in godliness ; there is yet time, the hour is not yet past.[1]

Why wilt thou defer thy good purpose from day to day? Arise and begin in this very instant, and say, Now is the time to be doing, now is the time to be striving, now is the fit time to amend myself.

When thou art ill at ease and much troubled, then is the time of deserving best.

Thou must pass through fire and water [2] before thou come to the place of refreshing.

Unless thou dost earnestly force thyself, thou shalt never get the victory over sin.

So long as we carry about us this frail body of ours, we can never be without sin, or live without weariness and pain.

We would gladly be quiet and freed from all misery, but seeing by sin we have lost our innocency, we have together with that lost also the true felicity.[3]

Therefore it becomes us to have patience, and to wait for the mercy of God, till this iniquity pass away, and mortality be swallowed up of life.[4]

VI. O how great is human frailty, which is always prone to evil.[5]

To-day thou confessest thy sins, and to-morrow thou committest the very same thou hast confessed.

Now, thou art purposed to look well unto thy ways, and within a while thou so behavest thyself, as though thou hadst never any such purpose at all.

Good cause have we therefore to humble ourselves,[6] and never to have any great conceit of ourselves : since we are so frail and so inconstant.

Besides, that may quickly be lost by our own negligence, which, by the grace of God, with much labour we have scarce at length obtained.

VII. What will become of us in the end, who begin so early to wax lukewarm !

---

[1] Rom. xiii. [11] ; Heb. x. [35]   [2] Psalm xlvi. [12].
[3] Rom. vii. [24] ; Gen. iii. [17].   [4] 2 Cor. v. [4].
[5] Gen. vi. [5] ; viii. [21].   [6] 2 Mac. ix. [11].

Woe be unto us, if we will so give ourselves unto ease, as if all were in peace and safety, when as yet there appeareth no sign of true holiness in our conversation !

We have much need like young beginners to be newly instructed again to good life, if haply there be some hope of future amendment, and greater proficiency in things spiritual.

CHAPTER XXIII

OF MEDITATION ON DEATH

VERY quickly there will be an end of thee here ;[1] look what will become of thee in another world.

To-day the man is here ; to-morrow he is gone.

And when he is out of sight, quickly also is he out of mind.

O the stupidity and hardness of man's heart, which thinketh only upon the present, and doth not rather care for what is to come !

Thou oughtest so to order thyself in all thy thoughts and actions, as if to-day thou wert about to die.[2]

If thou hadst a good conscience, thou wouldst not greatly fear death.[3]

It were better to avoid sin than to fly death.[4]

If to-day thou art not prepared, how wilt thou be so to-morrow.[5]

To-morrow is uncertain, and how knowest thou that thou shalt live till to-morrow !

II. What availeth it to live long, when there is so small amendment in our practice !

Alas ! length of days doth more often make our sins the greater, than our lives the better !

[1] Job ix. [25, 26] ; xiv. [1, 2] ; Luke xii. [20] ; Heb. ix. [27].
[2] Matt. xxv. [13].   [3] Luke xii. [37].
[4] Wisd. iv. [16].   [5] Matt. xxiv. [44] ; xxv. [10].

O that we had spent but one day in this world thoroughly well !

Many there are who count how long it is since their conversion ; and yet full slender oftentimes is the fruit of amendment of life.

. If to die be accounted dreadful, to live long may perhaps prove more dangerous.

Happy is he that always hath the hour of his death before his eyes,[1] and daily prepareth himself to die.

If at any time thou hast seen another man die, make account thou must also pass the same way.[2]

III. When it is morning, think thou mayest die before night ;

And when evening comes, dare not to promise thyself the next morning.

Be thou therefore always in a readiness, and so lead thy life that death may never take thee unprepared.[3]

Many die suddenly and when they look not for it ; for the Son of man will come at an hour when we think not.[4]

When that last hour shall come, thou wilt begin to have a far different opinion of thy whole life that is past, and be exceeding sorry thou hast been so careless and remiss.

IV. O how wise and happy is he that now laboureth to be such an one in his life, as he wisheth to be found at the hour of death !

A perfect contempt of the world,[5] a fervent desire to go forward in all virtue, the love of discipline, the painfulness of repentance, the readiness of obedience, the denying of ourselves, and the bearing any affliction whatever for the love of Christ, will give us great confidence we shall die happily.

Whilst thou art in health thou mayest do much good ; but when thou art sick, I see not what thou wilt be able to do.

Few by sickness grow better and more reformed ; as

[1] Eccles. vii. [1].   [2] Heb. ix. [27].
[3] Luke xxi. [36].   [4] Matt. xxiv. [44] ; Luke xii. [40].
[5] Ecclus. xli. [1].

also they who wander much abroad, seldom thereby become holy.

V. Trust not to friends and kindred, neither do thou put off the care of thy soul's welfare till hereafter; for men will forget thee, sooner than thou art aware of.

It is better to look to it betime, and do some good beforehand, than to trust to other men's help.[1]

If thou be not careful for thyself now, who will be careful for thee hereafter?

· The time that is now present is very precious: now are the days of salvation; now is the acceptable time.

But alas! that thou shouldest spend thy time so idly here, when thou mightest purchase to live eternally hereafter.

The time will come, when thou shalt desire one day or hour to amend in, and I cannot say that it will be granted thee.

VI. O beloved, from how great danger mightest thou deliver thyself, from how great fear free thyself, if thou wouldst be ever fearful and mindful of death!

Labour now so to live, that at the hour of death thou mayest rather rejoice than fear.

Learn now to die to the world, that thou mayest then begin to live with Christ.[2]

Learn now to contemn all things,[3] that thou mayest then freely go to Christ.

Chastise thy body now by repentance,[4] that thou mayest then have assured confidence.

VII. Ah! fool, why dost thou think to live long, when thou canst not promise to thyself one day.[5]

How many have been deceived and suddenly snatched away!

How often dost thou hear these reports, Such a man is slain, another man is drowned, a third breaks his neck with a fall from some high place, this man died eating, and that man playing!

[1] Isaiah xxx. [5]; xxxi. [1]; Jer. xvii. [5]; xlviii. [7]; Matt. vi. [20].

[2] Rom. vi. [1].   [3] Luke xiv. [33].

[4] 1 Cor. ix. [27].   [5] Luke xii. [20].

One perished by fire, another by the sword, another of the plague, another was slain by thieves. Thus death is the end of all, and man's life suddenly passeth away like a shadow.[1]

VIII. Who shall remember thee when thou art dead? and who shall pray for thee?

Do, do now, my beloved, whatsoever thou art able to do; for thou knowest not when thou shalt die, nor yet what shall befall thee after thy death.

Now whilst thou hast time, heap unto thyself everlasting riches.[2]

Think on nothing but the salvation of thy soul, care for nothing but the things of God.

Make now friends to thyself by honouring the Saints of God, and imitating their actions, that when thou failest in this life, they may receive thee into everlasting habitations.[3]

IX. Keep thyself as a stranger and pilgrim upon the earth,[4] and as one to whom the affairs of this world do nothing appertain.

Keep thy heart free, and lifted up to God, because thou hast here no abiding city.[5]

Send thither thy daily prayers and sighs together with thy tears, that after death thy spirit may be found worthy with much happiness to pass to the Lord. *Amen.*

CHAPTER XXIV

OF JUDGMENT, AND THE PUNISHMENT OF SINNERS

IN all things have a special aim to thy end, and how thou wilt be able to stand before that severe Judge[6] to whom nothing is hid, who is not pacified with gifts,

---

[1] Job xiv. [2].
[2] Matt. vi. [20]; Luke xii. [33]; Gal. vi. [8].
[3] Luke xvi. [9]; Heb. xi.   [4] 1 Pet. ii. [11].
[5] Heb. xiii. [14].   [6] Heb. x. [31].

nor admitteth any excuses, but will judge according to right and equity.

O wretched and foolish sinner, who sometimes fearest the countenance of an angry man, what answer wilt thou make to God who knoweth all thy wickedness![1]

Why dost thou not provide for thyself[2] against that great day of judgment, when no man can excuse or answer for another, but every one shall have enough to answer for himself!

Now are thy pains profitable, thy tears acceptable,[3] thy groans audible, thy grief pacifieth God, and purgeth thy soul.

II. The patient man hath a great and wholesome purgatory,[4] who though he receive injuries, yet grieveth more for the malice of another, than for his own wrong; who prayeth willingly for his adversaries,[5] and from his heart forgiveth their offences; he delayeth not to ask forgiveness of whomsoever he hath offended; he is sooner moved to compassion than to anger; he often offereth [an holy] violence to himself, and laboureth to bring the body wholly into subjection to the spirit.

It is better to purge out our sins, and cut off our vices here, than to keep them to be punished here-after.

Verily we do but deceive ourselves through an inordinate love of the flesh.

III. What is there that the infernal fire shall feed upon, but thy sins?

The more thou sparest thyself now and followest the flesh, the more severe hereafter shall be thy punishment, and thou storest up greater fuel for that flame.

In what things a man hath sinned, in the same shall he be the more grievously punished.

There shall the slothful be pricked forward with burning goads, and the glutton be tormented with extreme hunger and thirst.

[1] Job ix. [2].   [2] Luke xvi. [9].
[3] 2 Cor. vi. [4].   [4] James i. [4].
[5] Luke xxiii. [34]; Acts vii. [60].

There shall the luxurious and lovers of pleasures be bathed in burning pitch and stinking brimstone, and the envious, like mad dogs, shall howl for very grief.

IV. There is no sin but shall have its own proper torment.

There the proud shall be filled with all confusion ; the covetous shall be pinched with miserable penury ;

One hour of pain there shall be more bitter than a thousand years of the sharpest penance here !

There is no quiet, no comfort for the damned there ; [1] yet here we have some intermission of our labours, and enjoy the comfort of our friends.

Be now solicitous and sorrowful because of thy sins, that at the day of judgment thou mayest be secure with the company of blessed souls.

For then shall the righteous with great boldness stand against such as have vexed and oppressed them. [2]

Then shall he stand to judge them, who doth now humbly submit himself to the censures of men.

Then shall the poor and humble have great confidence, but the proud man shall be compassed with fear on every side.

V. Then will it appear that he was wise in this world, who had learned to be a fool and despised for Christ's sake.

Then shall every affliction patiently undergone delight us, when the mouth of all iniquity shall be stopped. [3]

Then shall all the devout rejoice, and all the profane mourn.

Then shall he more rejoice that hath beat down his own flesh, than he that hath abounded in all pleasure and delight. [4]

Then shall the poor attire shine gloriously, and the precious robes seem vile and contemptible.

Then the poor cottage shall be more commended, than the gilded palace.

---

[1] Job xl. [12], xli.   [2] Wisd. v. [1].
[3] Psalm cvii. [42].   [4] 2 Cor. iv. [17].

Then will constant patience more avail us, than all earthly power.

Then simple obedience shall be exalted above all worldly wisdom.[1]

VI. Then shall a good and clear conscience more rejoice a man, than all the learning of philosophy.

Then shall the contempt of riches weigh more than all the worldling's treasure.

Then wilt thou be more comforted that thou hast prayed devoutly, than that thou hast fared daintily.

Then wilt thou be more glad thou hast kept silence, than that thou hast talked much.

Then will good works avail more than many goodly words.

Then a strict life and severe repentance will be more pleasing than all earthly delights.

Accustom thyself now to suffer a little, that thou mayest then be delivered from more grievous pains.

Prove first here what thou canst endure hereafter.

If now thou canst endure so little, how wilt thou then be able to support eternal torments?

If now a little suffering make thee so impatient, what will hell fire do hereafter?

Assure thyself thou canst not have two paradises; it is impossible to enjoy delights in this world, and after that to reign with Christ.

VII. Suppose thou hast hitherto lived always in honours and delights, what would all this avail thee if thou wert to die at this instant?[2]

All therefore is vanity,[3] except to love God and serve Him only.

For he that loveth God with all his heart, is neither afraid of death, nor of punishment, nor of judgment, nor of hell; for perfect love gives secure access to God.[4]

But he that takes delight in sin, what marvel is it if he be afraid, both of death and judgment?

Yet it is good, although love be not yet of force to

---

[1] Isaiah xxix. [19].   [2] Luke xii. [20].
[3] Eccles. i. [2].   [4] Rom. viii. [39].

withhold thee from sin, that at least the fear of hell should restrain thee.

But he that layeth aside the fear of God, can never continue long in good estate, but falleth quickly into the snares of the devil.

CHAPTER XXV

OF THE ZEALOUS AMENDMENT OF OUR WHOLE LIFE

BE watchful and diligent in the service of God ;[1] and often bethink thyself wherefore thou camest hither, and why thou hast left the world. Was it not that thou mightest live to God, and become a spiritual man ?

Be fervent then in going forward,[2] for shortly thou shalt receive the reward of thy labours ; there shall not be then any more fear or sorrow in thy coasts.[3]

Labour but now a little, and thou shalt find great rest, yea, perpetual joy.[4]

If thou continuest faithful and fervent in thy work, no doubt but God will be faithful and liberal in rewarding thee.[5]

Thou oughtest to have a good hope[6] of getting the victory ; but thou must not be secure, lest thou wax either negligent or proud.

II. When one that was in anxiety of mind, often wavering between fear and hope, did once, being oppressed with grief, humbly prostrate himself in a church before the altar in prayer, and said within himself, O if I knew that I should yet persevere ! he presently heard within him an answer from God, which said, What if thou didst know it, what wouldest thou do ? Do now what thou wouldest do then, and thou shalt be secure.

And being herewith comforted and strengthened, he

---

[1] 2 Tim. iv. [5].   [2] Matt. v. [48].
[3] Rev. xxi. [4] ; xxii. [3].
[4] Ecclus. li. [27] ; Rev. xxi. [4] ; xxii. [3].
[5] Matt. xxv. [23].   [6] Rom. v. [5].

committed himself wholly to the will of God, and that noisome anxiety ceased :

Neither had he the mind to search curiously any farther, to know what should befall him ; but rather laboured to understand what was the perfect and acceptable will of God[1] for the beginning and accomplishing of every good work.

III. ' Hope in the Lord, and do good,' saith the Prophet, ' and inhabit the land, and thou shalt be fed in the riches thereof.'[2]

One thing there is that draweth many back from a spiritual progress, and the diligent amendment of their lives ; viz. Extreme fear of the difficulty, or the labour of the combat.

However, they above others improve most in all virtue, who endeavour most to overcome those things which are most grievous and contrary unto them.

For there a man improveth most and obtaineth greater grace, where he most overcometh himself and mortifieth himself in spirit.

IV. But all men have not equally much to overcome and mortify.

Yet he that is zealous and diligent, though he have more passions, shall profit more than another that is of a more temperate disposition, if he be less fervent in the pursuit of all virtue.

Two things especially much further our amendment, to wit, To withdraw ourselves violently from that to which nature is viciously inclined, and to labour earnestly for that good which we most want.

Be careful also to avoid with great diligence those things in thyself, which do commonly displease thee in others.

V. Gather some profit to thy soul wheresoever thou art ; so as if thou seest or hearest of any good examples, stir up thyself to the imitation thereof.

But if thou observe any thing worthy of reproof, beware thou do not the same. And if at any time thou hast done it, labour quickly to amend thyself.

[1] Rom. xii. [2].　　　　[2] Psalm xxxvii. [3].

As thine eye observeth others,[1] so art thou also noted again by others.

O how sweet and pleasant a thing it is, to see brethren fervent and devout, well-mannered and well-disciplined![2]

And on the contrary, how sad and grievous a thing it is, to see them live in a dissolute and disordered sort, not applying themselves to that for which they are called!

How hurtful a thing is it, when they neglect the good purposes of their vocation, and busy themselves in that which is not committed to their care!

VI. Be mindful of the profession thou hast made, and have always before the eyes of thy soul the remembrance of thy Saviour crucified.

Thou hast good cause to be ashamed in looking upon the life of JESUS Christ, seeing thou hast not as yet endeavoured to conform thyself more unto Him though thou hast been a long time in the way of God.

A religious person that exerciseth himself seriously and devoutly in the most holy life and passion of our Lord, shall there abundantly find whatsoever is necessary and profitable for him; neither shall he need to seek any better thing, out of JESUS.

O if JESUS crucified would come into our hearts,[3] how quickly and fully should we be taught!

VII. A fervent religious person taketh and beareth all well that is commanded him.

But he that is negligent and lukewarm, hath tribulation upon tribulation, and on all sides is afflicted; for he is void of inward consolation, and is forbidden to seek external comforts.

A religious person that liveth not according to discipline, lies open to great mischief to the ruin of his soul.

He that seeketh liberty and ease, shall ever live in disquiet; for one thing or other will displease him.

[1] Matt. vii. [3].
[2] Eph. v. [perhaps vi. 10—17]; 1 Cor. xii. [18]; Eccles. iii. [1].
[3] Gal. ii. [20]; vi. [14].

VIII. O that we had nothing else to do, but always with our mouth and whole heart to praise our Lord God !

O that thou mightest never have need to eat, or drink, or sleep ; but mightest always praise God, and only employ thyself in spiritual exercises ; thou shouldest then be much more happy than now thou art, when for so many necessities thou art constrained to serve thy body !

Would God there were not these necessities, but only the spiritual refreshments of the soul, which, alas, we taste of too seldom !

IX. When a man cometh to that estate, that he seeketh not his comfort from any creature, then doth he begin perfectly to relish God. Then shall he be contented with whatsoever doth befall him in this world.

Then shall he neither rejoice in great matters, nor be sorrowful for small ; but entirely and confidently commit himself to God, who shall be unto him all in all ;[1] to whom nothing doth perish nor die, but all things do live unto Him, and serve him at a beck without delay.

X. Remember always thy end,[2] and how that time lost never returns. Without care and diligence thou shalt never get virtue.

If thou begin to wax lukewarm,[3] it will begin to be evil with thee.

But if thou give thyself to fervour of spirit, thou shalt find much peace, and feel less labour, through the assistance of God's grace, and the love of virtue.

The fervent and diligent man is prepared for all things.

It is harder work to resist vices and passions, than to toil in bodily labours.

He that avoideth not small faults, by little and little falleth into greater.[4]

[1] Rom. xi. [36] ; 1 Cor. viii. [6] ; xii. [6] ; xv. [28].
[2] Ecclus. vii. [36].   [3] Rev. iii. [16].
[4] Ecclus. xix. [1].

Thou wilt always rejoice in the evening, if thou spend the day profitably.

Be watchful over thyself, stir up thyself, admonish thyself, and whatever becomes of others neglect not thyself.

The more violence thou usest against thyself, the greater shall be thy profiting. *Amen.*

THE SECOND BOOK

ADMONITIONS TENDING TO THINGS INTERNAL

CHAPTER I

OF THE INWARD LIFE

'THE Kingdom of God is within you,'[1] saith the Lord. Turn thee with thy whole heart[2] unto the Lord, and forsake this wretched world, and thy soul shall find rest.

Learn to despise outward things, and to give thyself to things inward, and thou shalt perceive the Kingdom of God to come in thee.

'For the Kingdom of God is peace and joy in the Holy Ghost,'[3] which is not given to the unholy.

Christ will come unto thee, and shew thee His own consolation, if thou prepare for Him a worthy mansion within thee.

All His glory and beauty is from within,[4] and there He delighteth Himself.

The inward man He often visiteth; and hath with him sweet discourses, pleasant solace, much peace, familiarity exceeding wonderful.

II. O faithful soul, make ready thy heart for this Bridegroom, that He may vouchsafe to come unto thee, and to dwell within thee.

For thus saith He, 'If any love Me, he will keep My words, and We will come unto him, and will make our abode with him.'[5]

[1] Luke xvii. [21].   [2] Joel ii. [12].   [3] Rom. xiv. [17].
[4] Psalm xiv. [13].   [5] John xiv. [23].

E

Give therefore admittance unto Christ, and deny entrance to all others.

When thou hast Christ, thou art rich, and hast enough.   He will be thy faithful and provident helper in all things, so as thou shalt not need to trust in men.

For men soon change, and quickly fail ; but Christ remaineth for ever,[1] and standeth by us firmly unto the end.

III. There is no great trust to be put in a frail and mortal man,[2] even though he be profitable and dear unto us : neither ought we to be much grieved, if sometimes he cross and contradict us.

They that to-day take thy part, to-morrow may be against thee ; and often do they turn right round like the wind.

Put all thy trust in God,[3] let Him be thy fear, and thy love : He shall answer for thee, and will do in all things what is best for thee.

Thou hast not here an abiding city ;[4] and wheresoever thou mayest be, thou art a stranger and pilgrim : neither shalt thou ever have rest, unless thou be most inwardly united unto Christ.

IV. Why dost thou here gaze about, since this is not the place of thy rest?   In Heaven ought to be thy home,[5] and all earthly things are to be looked upon as it were by the way.

All things pass away,[6] and thou together with them.

Beware thou cleave not unto them, lest thou be caught, and so perish.   Let thy thought be on the Highest, and thy prayer for mercy directed unto Christ without ceasing.

If thou canst not contemplate high and heavenly things, rest thyself in the passion of Christ, and dwell willingly in His sacred wounds.

For if thou fly devoutly unto the wounds and precious

---

[1] John xii. [34].   [2] Jer. xvii. [5].
[3] 1 Pet. v. [7].   [4] Heb. xiii. [14].
[5] Phil. iii. [20].   [6] Wisd. v. [9].

marks of the Lord JESUS, thou shalt feel great comfort in tribulation : neither wilt thou much care for the slights of men, and wilt easily bear words of detraction.

V. Christ was also in the world, despised of men, and in greatest necessity, forsaken by His acquaintance and friends, in the midst of slanders.[1]

Christ was willing to suffer and be despised ; and darest thou complain of any man ?

Christ had adversaries and backbiters ; and dost thou wish to have all men thy friends and benefactors ?

Whence shall thy patience attain her crown [2] if no adversity befall thee ?

If thou art willing to suffer no opposition, how wilt thou be the friend of Christ ?

Suffer with Christ, and for Christ, if thou desire to reign with Christ.

VI. If thou hadst but once perfectly entered into the secrets of the Lord JESUS, and tasted a little of His ardent love ; then wouldest thou not regard thine own convenience or inconvenience, but rather wouldest rejoice at slanders, if they should be cast upon thee ; for the love of JESUS maketh a man despise himself.

A lover of JESUS and of the truth, and a true inward Christian, and one free from inordinate affections, can freely turn himself unto God, and lift himself above himself in spirit, and with joy remain at rest.

VII. He that judgeth of all things as they are, and not as they are said or esteemed to be, is truly wise, and taught rather of God than men.[3]

He that can live inwardly, and make small reckoning of things without, neither requireth places, nor expecteth times, for performing of religious exercises.

A spiritual man quickly recollecteth himself, because he never poureth out himself wholly to outward things.

He is not hindered by outward labour, or business, which may be necessary for the time : but as things fall out, so he accommodates himself to them.

[1] Matt. xii. [24] ; xvi. [21] ; John xv. [20].
[2] 2 Tim. ii. [5].   [3] Isaiah liv. [13].

He that is well ordered and disposed within himself, cares not for the strange and perverse behaviour of men.

A man is hindered and distracted, in proportion as he draweth external matters unto himself.

VIII. If it were well with thee, and thou wert well purified from sin, all things would fall out to thee for good,[1] and to thy advancement.

But many things displease and often trouble thee; because thou art not yet perfectly dead unto thyself, nor separated from all earthly things.

Nothing so defileth and entangleth the heart of man, as the impure love to creatures.

If thou refuse outward comfort, thou wilt be able to contemplate the things of Heaven, and often to receive internal joy.

CHAPTER II

OF HUMBLE SUBMISSION

REGARD not much who is for thee, or against thee;[2] but mind what thou art about, and take care that God may be with thee in every thing thou doest.

Have a good conscience, and God will well defend thee.[3]

For whom God will help, no man's perverseness shall be able to hurt.

If thou canst be silent and suffer, without doubt thou shalt see that the Lord will help thee.

He knoweth the time and manner how to deliver thee, and therefore thou oughtest to resign thyself unto Him.

It belongs to God to help, and to deliver from all confusion.

It is often very profitable, to keep us more humble, that others know and rebuke our faults.

---

[1] Rom. viii. [28].   [2] Rom. viii. [31]; 1 Cor. iv. [3].
         [3] Psalm xxviii. [7].

11. When a man humbleth himself for his failings, then he easily pacifieth others, and quickly satisfieth those that are offended with him.

God protecteth the humble and delivereth him;[1] the humble He loveth and comforteth; unto the humble man He inclineth Himself; unto the humble He giveth great grace; and after his humiliation He raiseth him to glory.

Unto the humble He revealeth His secrets,[2] and sweetly draweth and inviteth him unto Himself.

The humble person, though he suffer confusion, is yet tolerably well in peace; for that he resteth on God, and not on the world.

Do not think that thou hast made any progress, unless thou esteem thyself inferior to all.

CHAPTER III

OF A GOOD PEACEABLE MAN

First, keep thyself in peace, and then shalt thou be able to pacify others.

A peaceable man doth more good than he that is well learned.

A passionate man draweth even good into evil, and easily believeth the worst.

A good peaceable man turneth all things to good.

He that is well in peace, is not suspicious of any.[3] But he that is discontented and troubled, is tossed with divers suspicions: he is neither quiet himself, nor suffereth others to be quiet.

He often speaketh that which he ought not to speak; and omitteth that which were more expedient for him to do.

He considereth what others are bound to do,[4] and neglecteth that which he is bound to himself.

[1] James iii. [perhaps iv. 6]; Job v. [11].
[2] Matt. xi. [25].   [3] 1 Cor. xiii. [5].
[4] Matt. vii. [3].

First therefore have a careful zeal over thyself,[1] and then thou mayest justly shew thyself zealous also of thy neighbour's good.

II. Thou knowest well how to excuse and colour thine own deeds, but thou art not willing to receive the excuses of others.

It were more just that thou shouldest accuse thyself, and excuse thy brother.

If thou wilt be borne withal, bear also with another.[2]

Behold, how far off thou art yet from true charity and humility ; for that knows not how to be angry with any, or to be moved with indignation, but only against one's self.

It is no great matter to associate with the good, and gentle ; for this is naturally pleasing to all, and every one willingly enjoyeth peace, and loveth those best that agree with him.

But to be able to live peaceably with hard, and perverse persons, or with the disorderly, or with such as go contrary to us, is a great grace, and a most commendable and manly thing.

III. Some there are that keep themselves in peace, and are in peace also with others.

And there are some that neither are in peace themselves, nor suffer others to be in peace : they are troublesome to others, but always more troublesome to themselves.

And others there are that keep themselves in peace, and study to bring others unto peace.

Nevertheless, our whole peace in this miserable life consisteth rather in humble sufferance, than in not feeling adversities.

He that can best tell how to suffer, will best keep himself in peace. That man is conqueror of himself, and lord of the world, the friend of Christ, and heir of Heaven.

[1] Acts i. [perhaps xxii. 3].
[2] Gal. vi. [2] ; 1 Cor. xiii. [7].

CHAPTER IV

OF A PURE MIND, AND SIMPLE INTENTION

By two wings, a man is lifted up from things earthly, namely, by Simplicity and Purity.

Simplicity ought to be in our intention ; Purity in our affections.   Simplicity doth tend towards God ; Purity doth apprehend and taste Him.

No good action will hinder thee, if thou be inwardly free from inordinate affection.

If thou intend and seek nothing else but the will of God and the good of thy neighbour, thou shalt thoroughly enjoy internal liberty.

If thy heart were sincere and upright, then every creature would be unto thee a looking-glass of life, and a book of holy doctrine.

There is no creature so small and abject, that it representeth not the goodness of God.[1]

II.   If thou wert inwardly good and pure,[2] then wouldest thou be able to see and understand all things well without impediment.

A pure heart penetrateth Heaven and hell.

Such as every one is inwardly, so he judgeth outwardly.

If there be joy in the world, surely a man of a pure heart possesseth it.

And if there be any where tribulation and affliction, an evil conscience best knows it.

As iron put into the fire loseth its rust, and becometh clearly red hot, so he that wholly turneth himself unto God, puts off all slothfulness, and is transformed into a new man.

III.   When a man beginneth to grow lukewarm, then he is afraid of a little labour, and willingly receiveth external comfort.

But when he once beginneth to overcome himself

[1] Rom. i. [20].
[2] Prov. iii. [3, 4] ; Psalm cxix. [100].

perfectly, and to walk manfully in the way of God; then he esteemeth those things to be light which before seemed grievous unto him.

CHAPTER V

OF THE CONSIDERATION OF ONE'S SELF

WE cannot trust much to ourselves,[1] because grace oftentimes is wanting to us, and understanding also.

There is but little light in us, and that which we have we quickly lose by our negligence.

Oftentimes too we do not perceive our own inward blindness how great it is.

We often do evil, and excuse it worse.[2]

We are sometimes moved with passion, and we think it to be zeal.

We reprehend small things in others, and pass over greater matters in ourselves.[3]

We quickly enough feel and weigh what we suffer at the hands of others; but we mind not what others suffer from us.

He that well and rightly considereth his own works, will find little cause to judge hardly of another.

II. The inward Christian preferreth the care of himself before all other cares.[4]   And he that diligently attendeth unto himself, can easily keep silence concerning others.

Thou wilt never be thus inwardly religious, unless thou pass over other men's matters with silence, and look especially to thyself.

It thou attend wholly unto God and thyself, thou wilt be but little moved with whatsoever thou seest abroad.[5]

Where art thou, when thou art not with thyself?

---

[1] Jer. xvii. [5].   [2] Psalm cxli. [4].
[3] Matt. vii. [5].   [4] Matt. xvi. [26].
[5] 1 Cor. iv. [3]; Gal. i. [10].

And when thou hast run over all, what hast thou then profited, if thou hast neglected thyself.

If thou desirest peace of mind and true unity of purpose, thou must still put all things behind thee, and look only upon thyself.

III. Thou shalt then make great progress, if thou keep thyself free from all temporal care.

Thou shalt greatly fall back, if thou esteem temporal any thing.

Let nothing be great unto thee, nothing high, nothing pleasing, nothing acceptable, but only God Himself, or that which is of God.

Esteem all comfort vain,[1] which thou receivest from any creature.

A soul that loveth God, despiseth all things that are inferior unto God.

God alone is everlasting, and of infinite greatness, filling all creatures ; the soul's solace, and the true joy of the heart.

CHAPTER VI

OF THE JOY OF A GOOD CONSCIENCE

THE glory of a good man, is the testimony of a good conscience.[2]

Have a good conscience, and thou shalt ever have joy.

A good conscience is able to bear very much, and is very cheerful in adversities.

An evil conscience is always fearful and unquiet.[3]

Thou shalt rest sweetly, if thy heart do not reprehend thee.

Never rejoice, but when thou hast done well.

Sinners have never true joy, nor feel inward peace ; because 'There is no peace to the wicked,' saith the Lord.[4]

---

[1] Eccles. i. [14]. [2] 1 Cor. i. [31].
[3] Wisd. xvii. [11]. [4] Isaiah lvii. [21].

And if they should say, 'We are in peace, no evil shall fall upon us,[1] and who shall dare to hurt us?' believe them not; for upon a sudden will arise the wrath of God, and their deeds shall be brought to nought, and their thoughts shall perish.

II. To glory in tribulation, is no hard thing for him that loveth; for so to glory, is to glory in the Cross of the Lord.[2]

That glory is short, which is given and received from men.[3]

Sorrow always accompanieth the world's glory.

The glory of the good is in their consciences, and not in the tongues of men. The gladness of the just is of God,[4] and in God; and their joy is of the Truth.

He that desireth true and everlasting glory, careth not for that which is temporal.

And he that seeketh temporal glory, or despiseth it not from his soul, sheweth himself to have but little esteem of the glory of Heaven.

He enjoyeth great tranquillity of heart, that careth neither for the praises, nor dispraises of men.

III. He will easily be content and pacified, whose conscience is pure.

Thou art not the more holy, though thou be commended; nor the more worthless, though thou be found fault with.

What thou art, that thou art; neither by words canst thou be made greater, than what thou art in the sight of God.

If thou consider what thou art within thee, thou wilt not care what men talk of thee.

Man looketh on the countenance, but God on the heart.[5] Man considereth the deeds, but God weigheth the intentions.

To be always doing well, and to esteem little of one's self, is the sign of an humble soul

[1] Luke xii. [19].
[2] Rom. viii. [perhaps v. 3]; Gal. vi. [14].
[3] John v. [44].   [4] 2 Cor. iii. [5].
[5] 1 Sam. xvi. [7].

To refuse to be comforted by any creature, is a sign of great purity, and inward confidence.

IV. He that seeketh no witness for himself from without, doth shew that he hath wholly committed himself unto God.

'For not he that commendeth himself, the same is approved, (saith Saint Paul,) but whom God commendeth.'[1]

To walk inwardly with God, and not to be kept abroad by any outward affection, is the state of a spiritual man.

CHAPTER VII

OF THE LOVE OF JESUS ABOVE ALL THINGS

Blessed is he that understandeth[2] what it is to love Jesus, and to despise himself for Jesus' sake.

Thou oughtest to leave [thy] beloved, for [thy] Beloved ;[3] for that Jesus will be loved alone above all things.

The love of things created is deceitful and inconstant ; the love of Jesus is faithful and persevering.

He that cleaveth unto creatures, shall fall with that which is subject to fall ; he that embraceth Jesus shall stand firmly for ever.

Love Him, and keep Him for thy friend, who when all go away, will not forsake thee, nor suffer thee to perish in the end.

Some time or other thou must be separated from all, whether thou wilt or no.

II. Keep close to Jesus both in life and in death, and commit thyself unto His trust, who, when all fail, can alone help thee.

Thy Beloved is of that nature, that He will admit of

[1] 2 Cor. x. [18].   [2] Psalm cxix. [1, 2].
[3] Deut. vi. [5] ; Matt. xxii. [37].

no rival ; but will have thy heart alone, and sit on His own throne as King.

If thou couldest empty thyself perfectly from all creatures, Jesus would willingly dwell with thee.

Whatsoever thou reposest in men, out of Jesus, is all little better than lost.

Trust not nor lean upon a reed full of wind ; for that all flesh is grass, and all the glory thereof shall wither away as the flower of the field.[1]

III. Thou shalt quickly be deceived, if thou only look to the outward appearance of men.

For if in others thou seekest thy comfort and profit, thou shalt too often feel loss.

If thou seekest Jesus in all things, thou shalt surely find Jesus.

But if thou seekest thyself, thou shalt also find thyself, but to thine own destruction.

For man doth more hurt himself if he seek not Jesus, than the whole world and all his adversaries [could injure him].

CHAPTER VIII

OF FAMILIAR CONVERSE WITH JESUS

When Jesus is present, all is well, and nothing seems difficult ; but when Jesus is absent, every thing is hard.

When Jesus speaks not inwardly to us, all other comfort is nothing worth ; but if Jesus speak but one word, we feel great consolation.

Did not Mary Magdalene rise immediately from the place where she wept, when Martha said to her, 'The Master is come, and calleth for thee ?'[2]

Happy hour ! when Jesus calleth from tears to spiritual joy.

How dry and hard art thou without Jesus! How

[1] Isaiah xl. [6].   [2] John xi. [28].

foolish and vain, if thou desire any thing out of JESUS!

Is not this a greater loss, than if thou shouldest lose the whole world?[1]

II. What can the world profit thee without JESUS?

To be without JESUS is a grievous hell; and to be with JESUS, a sweet paradise.

If JESUS be with thee, no enemy shall be able to hurt thee.[2]

He that findeth JESUS, findeth a good treasure;[3] yea, a Good above all good.

And he that loseth JESUS, loseth much indeed, yea, more than the whole world!

Most poor is he who liveth without JESUS;[4] and he most rich who is well with JESUS.

III. It is matter of great skill to know how to hold converse with JESUS; and to know how to keep JESUS, a point of great wisdom.

Be thou humble and peaceable, and JESUS will be with thee.[5]

Be devout and quiet, and JESUS will stay with thee.

Thou mayest soon drive away JESUS, and lose His favour, if thou wilt turn aside to outward things.

And if thou shouldest drive Him from thee, and lose Him, unto whom wilt thou flee, and whom wilt thou then seek for thy friend?

Without a friend thou canst not well live; and if JESUS be not above all a friend to thee, thou shalt be indeed sad and desolate.

Thou actest therefore like an idiot, if thou trust or rejoice in any other.[6]

It is preferable to have all the world against us, rather than to have JESUS offended with us.

Amongst all therefore that be dear unto us, let JESUS alone be specially beloved.

IV. Love all for JESUS, but JESUS for Himself.

[1] Matt. xvi. [26].	[2] Rom. viii. [35]
[3] Matt. xiii. [44].	[4] Luke xii. [21].
[5] Prov. iii. [17].	[6] Gal. vi. [14].

Jesus Christ alone is singularly to be beloved ; who alone is found Good and Faithful above all friends.

For Him, and in Him, let as well friends as foes be dear unto thee ; and all these are to be prayed for, that He would make them all to know and love Him.[1]

Never desire to be singularly commended or beloved, for that appertaineth only unto God, who hath none like unto Himself.

Neither do thou desire that the heart of any should be set on thee, nor do thou set thy heart on the love of any ; but let Jesus be in thee, and in every good man.

V. Be pure and free within, and entangle not thy heart with any creature.

Thou oughtest to be naked and open before God, ever carrying thy heart pure towards Him, if thou wouldest be free to consider and see how sweet the Lord is.

And truly, unless thou be prevented and drawn by His grace, thou shalt never attain to that happiness to forsake and take leave of all, that thou alone mayest be united to Him alone.

For when the grace of God cometh unto a man, then he is made able for all things. And when It goeth away, then is he poor and weak, and as it were left only for the lash and scourge.

In this case thou oughtest not to be dejected, nor to despair ; but at God's will to stand steadily, and whatever comes upon thee, to endure it for the glory of Jesus Christ ; for after winter followeth summer, after night the day returneth, and after a tempest a great calm.

[1] Matt. v. [44] ; Luke vi. [27, 28].

CHAPTER IX

OF THE WANT OF ALL COMFORT

IT is no hard matter to despise human comfort, when we have divine.

It is much and very much, to be able to want both human and divine comfort;[1] and, for God's honour, to be willing cheerfully to endure banishment of heart; and to seek himself in nothing, nor to regard his own merit.

What great matter is it, if at the coming of Grace thou be cheerful and devout? this hour is wished for of all men.

He rideth easily enough whom the grace of God carrieth.

And what marvel if he feel not his burden, who is borne up by the Almighty, and led by the Sovereign Guide?

II. We are always willing to have something for our comfort; and a man doth not without difficulty strip himself of self.

The holy martyr Laurence with his priest, overcame the world, because whatsoever seemed delightsome in the world he despised; and for the love of Christ he patiently suffered God's chief Priest Sixtus, whom he most dearly loved, to be even taken away from him.

He therefore overcame the love of man by the love of the Creator; and he rather chose what pleased God, than human comfort.

So also do thou learn to part even with a near and dear friend, for the love of God.

Nor do thou take it hard, when thou art deserted by a friend, as knowing that we all at last must be separated one from another.

III. A man must strive long and mightily within himself, before he can learn fully to master himself, and to draw his whole heart into God.

[1] Phil. ii. [12].

When a man trusteth in himself, he easily slideth unto human comforts.

But a true lover of Christ, and a diligent follower of all virtue, does not fall back on comforts, nor seek such sensible sweetnesses; but rather prefers hard exercises, and to sustain severe labours for Christ.

IV. When therefore spiritual comfort is given thee from God, receive it with thankfulness; but understand that it is the gift of God, nor any desert of thine.

Be not puffed up, be not too joyful nor vainly presumptuous; but rather be the more humble for that gift, more wary too and fearful in all thine actions; for that hour will pass away, and temptation will follow.

When consolation is taken from thee, do not immediately despair; but with humility and patience wait for the heavenly visitation; for God is able to give thee back again more ample consolation.

This is nothing new nor strange unto them that have experience in the way of God; for the great Saints and ancient Prophets had oftentimes experience of such kind of vicissitudes.

.V. For which cause, one under the enjoyment of divine Grace, said, 'I said in my prosperity, I shall never be moved.' [1]

But in the want of this Grace, what he found in himself he goes on thus to speak of, 'Thou didst turn Thy face from me, and I was troubled.'

Yet in the midst of all this he doth not by any means despair, but more earnestly beseecheth the Lord, and saith, 'Unto Thee, O Lord, will I cry, and I will pray unto my God.'

At length, he receives the fruit of his prayer, and testifies that he was heard, saying, 'The Lord hath heard me, and taken pity on me; the Lord is become my helper.'

But wherein? 'Thou hast turned,' saith he, 'my sorrow into joy, and Thou hast compassed me about with gladness.'

[1] Psalm xxx. [6—11].

If great Saints were so dealt with, we that are weak and poor ought not to despair, if we be sometimes fervent and sometimes cold; for the Spirit cometh and goeth, according to the good pleasure of His own will.[1] For which cause blessed Job saith, 'Thou visitest him early in the morning, and suddenly Thou provest him.'[2]

VI. Whereupon then can I hope, or wherein ought I to trust, save in the great mercy of God alone, and in the only hope of heavenly grace?

For whether I have with me good men, either religious brethren, or faithful friends; whether holy books, or beautiful treatises, or sweet psalms and hymns; all these help but little, and have but little savour, when Grace forsaketh me, and I am left in mine own poverty.

At such time there is no better remedy than patience, and the denying of myself according to the will of God.[3]

VII. I never found any so religious and devout, that he had not sometimes a withdrawing of grace, or felt not some decrease of zeal.

There was never Saint so highly rapt and illuminated, who first or last was not tempted.

For he is not worthy of the high contemplation of God, who hath not been exercised with some tribulation for God's sake.

For temptation going before, is wont to be a sign of ensuing comfort.

For unto those that are proved by temptations, heavenly comfort is promised. 'He that shall overcome,' saith He, 'I will give him to eat of the Tree of life.'[4]

VIII. But divine consolation is given, that a man may be bolder to bear adversities.

There followeth also temptation, lest he should wax proud of any good.

[1] John iii. [8].   [2] Job vii. [18].
[3] Luke ix. [23].   [4] Rev. ii. [7].

F

The devil sleepeth not,[1] neither is the flesh as yet dead ; therefore cease not to prepare thyself to the battle ; for on thy right hand and on thy left are enemies who never rest.

CHAPTER X

OF GRATITUDE FOR THE GRACE OF GOD

Why seekest thou rest, since thou art born to labour ?[2]

Dispose thyself to patience rather than to comfort, and to the bearing of the Cross, rather than to gladness.[3]

What secular person is there that would not willingly receive spiritual joy and comfort, if he could always have it ?

For spiritual comforts exceed all the delights of the world, and pleasures of the flesh.

For all worldly delights are either vain or unclean ; but spiritual delights are only pleasant and honest, sprung from virtue, and infused by God into pure minds.

But no man can always enjoy these divine comforts according to his desire ; for the time of temptation is not long away.

II. But false freedom of mind and great confidence of ourselves is very contrary to heavenly visitations.

God doth well for us in giving the grace of comfort ; but man doth evil in not returning all again unto God with thanksgiving.

And therefore the gifts of Grace cannot flow in us, because we are unthankful to the Giver, and return them not wholly to the Head fountain.[4]

For Grace ever attendeth him that is duly thankful ; and from the proud shall be taken that which is wont to be given to the humble.

[1] 1 Pet. v. [8].   [2] Job v. [7].
[3] Luke xiv. [27].   [4] Ecclus. i. [5].

III. I desire not that consolation that taketh from me compunction ; nor do I affect that contemplation which leadeth to haughtiness of mind.

For all that is high, is not holy ; nor all that is sweet, good ; nor every desire, pure ; nor is everything that is dear unto us, pleasing to God.

Willingly do I accept of that grace, whereby I may ever be found more humble, and more affected with fear, and may become more ready to renounce myself.

He that is taught by the gift of Grace, and schooled by the scourge of the withdrawing thereof, will not dare to attribute any good to himself, but will rather acknowledge himself poor and naked.

Give unto God that which is God's,[1] and ascribe unto thyself that which is thine own ; that is, give thanks to God for His grace ; and acknowledge that to thyself alone is to be attributed sin, and the punishment due to sin.

IV. Set thyself always in the lowest place[2] and the highest shall be given thee ; for the highest cannot stand without the lowest.

The chiefest Saints before God, are the least in their own judgments ; and the more glorious they are, so much the humbler within themselves.

Those that are full of truth and heavenly glory, are not desirous of vain-glory.

Those that are firmly settled and grounded in God, can no way be proud.

And they that ascribe all unto God, what good soever they have received, seek not glory one of another, but wish for that glory which is from God alone ; and desire above all things that God may be praised in Himself, and in all His Saints ; and are always tending to this very thing.

V. Be therefore thankful for the least gift, so shalt thou be meet to receive greater.

Let the least be unto thee even as the greatest, yea the most contemptible gift as of especial value.

If thou consider the worth of the Giver, no gift will

---

[1] Matt. xxii. [21].   [2] Luke xiv. [10].

seem little, or of too mean esteem.   For that cannot be little which is given by the Most High God.

Yea, if He should give punishment and stripes, it ought to be matter of thankfulness ; because He doth it always for our welfare, whatsoever He permitteth to happen unto us.

He that desireth to keep the grace of God, let him be thankful for grace given, and patient for the taking away thereof : let him pray that it may return : let him be cautious and humble, lest he lose it.

CHAPTER XI

HOW FEW ARE THE LOVERS OF THE CROSS OF JESUS

JESUS hath now many lovers of His heavenly kingdom, but few bearers of His Cross.

He hath many desirous of consolation, but few of tribulation.

He findeth many companions of His table, but few of His abstinence.

All desire to rejoice with Him, few are willing to endure any thing for Him, or with Him.

Many follow JESUS unto the breaking of bread ; but few to the drinking of the cup of His Passion.[1]

Many reverence His miracles, few follow the ignominy of His Cross.

Many love JESUS so long as no adversities befall them.

Many praise and bless Him, so long as they receive any consolations from Him.

But if JESUS hide Himself, and leave them but a little while ; they fall either into complaining, or into too much dejection of mind.

II. But they who love JESUS for the sake of JESUS, and not for some special comfort of their own, bless

---

[1] Luke ix. [14] ; xxii. [41, 42].

Him in all tribulation and anguish of heart, as well as in the state of highest comfort.

Yea although He should never be willing to give them comfort, they notwithstanding would ever praise Him, and wish to be always giving thanks.

III. O how powerful is the pure love of JESUS, which is mixed with no self-interest, or self-love!

Are not all those to be called mercenary, who are ever seeking consolations?

Do they not shew themselves to be rather lovers of themselves than of Christ, who are always thinking of their own profit and advantage?[1]

Where shall one be found who is willing to serve God for nought?

IV. Rarely is any one found so spiritual as to be stript of all things.

For where is any man to be found that is indeed poor in spirit, and thoroughly void of all affection of creatures? 'From afar, yea from the ends of the earth, is his value.'[2]

If a man should give all his substance, yet is it nothing.

And if he should practise great repentance, still it is little.

And if he should attain to all knowledge, he is still afar off.

And if he should be of great virtue, and of very fervent devotion, yet there is much wanting: especially, one thing, which is most necessary for him.

What is that? That leaving all, he forsake himself, and go wholly from himself,[3] and retain nothing out of self-love.

And when he hath done all that is to be done, so far as he knoweth, let him think that he hath done nothing.

V. Let him not weigh that much, which might be much esteemed; but let him pronounce himself to be in truth an unprofitable servant, as the Truth Himself

[1] Phil. ii. [21].   [2] Prov. xxxi. [10. Latin version].
[3] Matt. xvi. [24].

saith, 'When you shall have done all things that are commanded you, say, We are unprofitable servants.'[1]

Then may he be truly poor and naked in spirit, and say with the Prophet, 'I am alone and poor.'[2]

Yet no man richer than he, no man more powerful, no man more free; for he is able to leave himself and all things, and to set himself in the lowest place.

CHAPTER XII.

OF THE KING'S HIGH WAY OF THE HOLY CROSS

Unto many this seemeth an hard speech, 'Deny thyself, take up thy cross, and follow Jesus.'[3]

But much harder will it be to hear that last word, 'Depart from Me, ye cursed, into everlasting fire.'[4]

For they who now willingly hear and follow the word of the Cross, shall not then fear[5] to hear the sentence of everlasting damnation.

This sign of the Cross shall be in the Heaven, when the Lord shall come to judgment.

Then all the servants of the Cross, who in their lifetime conformed themselves unto Christ crucified, shall draw near unto Christ the Judge with great confidence.

II. Why therefore fearest thou to take up the Cross which leadeth thee to a kingdom?

In the Cross is salvation, in the Cross is life, in the Cross is protection against our enemies, in the Cross is infusion of heavenly sweetness, in the Cross is strength of mind, in the Cross joy of spirit, in the Cross the height of virtue, in the Cross the perfection of sanctity.

There is no salvation of the soul, nor hope of everlasting life, but in the Cross.

Take up therefore thy Cross and follow Jesus,[6] and

[1] Luke xvii. [10].   [2] Psalm xxv. [16].
[3] Matt. xvi. [24].   [4] Matt. xxv. [41].
[5] Psalm cxii. [7].   [6] Luke xiv. [27].

thou shalt go into life everlasting. He went before, bearing His Cross,[1] and died for thee on the Cross; that thou mayest also bear thy Cross and desire to die on the Cross with Him.

For if thou be dead with Him, thou shalt also live with Him. And if thou be His companion in punishment, thou shalt be partaker with Him also in glory.[2]

III. Behold! in the Cross all doth consist, and all lieth in our dying thereon; for there is no other way unto life, and unto true inward peace, but the way of the holy Cross, and of daily mortification.

Go where thou wilt, seek whatsoever thou wilt, thou shalt not find a higher way above, nor a safer way below, than the way of the holy Cross.

Dispose and order all things according to thy will and judgment; yet thou shalt ever find, that of necessity thou must suffer somewhat, either willingly or against thy will, and so thou shalt ever find the Cross.

For either thou shalt feel pain in thy body, or in thy soul thou shalt suffer tribulation of spirit.

IV. Sometimes thou shalt be forsaken of God, sometimes thou shalt be troubled by thy neighbours; and, what is more, oftentimes thou shalt be wearisome to thyself.

Neither canst thou be delivered or eased by any remedy or comfort; but so long as it pleaseth God, thou oughtest to bear it.

For God will have thee learn to suffer tribulation without comfort; and that thou subject thyself wholly to Him, and by tribulation become more humble.

No man hath so cordial a feeling of the Passion of Christ, as he who hath suffered the like himself.

The Cross therefore is always ready, and every where waits for thee.

Thou canst not escape it whithersoever thou runnest; for wheresoever thou goest, thou carriest thyself with thee, and shalt ever find thyself.

Both above and below, without and within, which

---

[1] John xix. [17].   [2] 2 Cor. i. [5].

way soever thou dost turn thee, every where thou shalt find the Cross; and every where of necessity thou must hold fast patience, if thou wilt have inward peace, and enjoy an everlasting crown.

V. If thou bear the Cross cheerfully, it will bear thee, and lead thee to the desired end, namely, where there shall be an end of suffering, though here there shall not be.

If thou bear it unwillingly, thou makest for thyself a burden, and increasest thy load, and yet notwithstanding thou must bear it.

If thou cast away one cross, without doubt thou shalt find another, and that perhaps a more heavy one.

VI. Thinkest thou to escape that which no mortal man could ever avoid? Which of the Saints in the world was without crosses, and tribulation?

For not even our Lord Jesus Christ was ever one hour without the anguish of His Passion, so long as He lived. 'Christ' (saith He) 'must needs suffer, and rise again from the dead, and so enter into His glory.'[1] And how dost thou seek any other way than this royal way, which is the way of the holy Cross?

VII. Christ's whole life was a Cross and Martyrdom: and dost thou seek rest and joy for thyself?

Thou art deceived, thou art deceived if thou seek any other thing than to suffer tribulations; for this whole mortal life is full of miseries,[2] and signed on every side with crosses.

And the higher a person hath advanced in the Spirit, so much the heavier crosses he oftentimes findeth; because the grief of his banishment increases with his love to God.

VIII. Nevertheless this man, though so many ways afflicted, is not without refreshing comfort, for that he perceiveth very much benefit to accrue unto him by the enduring of his own cross.

For whilst he willingly putteth himself under it, all the burden of tribulation is turned into the confidence of Divine comfort.

[1] Luke xxiv. [26].   [2] Job vii. [1].

And the more the flesh is wasted by affliction, so much the more is the spirit strengthened by inward grace.

And sometimes he is so comforted with the desire of tribulation and adversity, for the love of conformity to the Cross of Christ, that he would not wish to be without grief and tribulation ;[1] because he believes that he shall be unto God so much the more acceptable, the more, and the more grievous things he can suffer for Him.

This is not the power of man, but it is the grace of Christ, which can and doth so much in frail flesh ; so that what naturally it always abhors and flees from, that by fervour of spirit it encounters and loves.

IX. It is not according to man's inclination to bear the Cross, to love the Cross, to chastise the body, and bring it into subjection, to flee honours, willingly to suffer contumelies, to despise himself and to wish to be despised, to endure all adversities and damages, and to desire no prosperity in this world.

If thou look to thyself, thou shalt be able of thyself to accomplish nothing of this kind.[2]

But if thou trust in the Lord, fortitude shall be given thee from Heaven, and the world and the flesh shall be made subject to thy command.

Neither shalt thou fear thy enemy the devil, if thou be armed with faith, and signed with the Cross of Christ.

X. Set thyself therefore, like a good and faithful servant of Christ, to bear manfully the Cross of thy Lord, who out of love was crucified for thee.

Prepare thyself to bear many adversities and divers kinds of troubles in this miserable life ; for so it will be with thee, wheresoever thou art, and so surely thou shalt find it, wheresoever thou hide thyself.

So it must be ; nor is there any remedy or means to escape from tribulation and sorrow, but only to endure thyself.

Drink of the Lord's cup[3] with hearty affection, if thou desire to be His friend, and to have part with Him.

[1] 2 Cor. iv. [16] ; xi. [23—30].   [2] 2 Cor. iii. [5].
[3] Matt. xx. [23] ; John xviii. [11].

As for comforts, leave them to God; let Him do therein as shall best please Him.

But do thou set thyself to suffer tribulations, and account them the greatest comforts; for the sufferings of this present time, although thou alone couldest suffer them all, cannot worthily deserve the glory which is to come.

XI. When thou shalt come to this estate, that tribulation[1] shall seem sweet, and thou shalt relish it for Christ's sake; then think it to be well with thee, for thou hast found a Paradise upon earth.

As long as it is grievous to thee to suffer, and that thou desirest to flee it, so long shalt thou be ill at ease, and the desire of escaping tribulation will follow thee every where.

XII. If thou dost set thyself to that thou oughtest, namely, to suffering, and to death, it will quickly be better with thee, and thou shalt find peace.

Although thou shouldest have been rapt even unto the third heaven with Paul,[2] thou art not for this secured that thou shalt suffer no adversity. 'I will shew him' (saith JESUS) 'how great things he must suffer for My Name.'[3]

It remaineth therefore, that thou suffer, if it please thee to love JESUS, and to serve Him perpetually.

XIII. O that thou wert worthy to suffer something for the Name of JESUS![4]   How great glory would remain unto thyself; what joy would arise to all God's Saints; how great edification also to thy neighbour!

For all men recommend patience; few, however, they are who are willing to suffer.

With great reason oughtest thou cheerfully to suffer some little for Christ's sake; since many suffer more grievous things for the world.

XIV. Know for certain, that thou oughtest to lead a dying life.[5]   And the more any man dieth to himself, so much the more doth he begin to live unto God.

[1] Rom. v. [3]; Gal. vi. [14].   [2] 2 Cor. xii. [4].
[3] Acts ix. [16].   [4] Acts v. [41].
            [5] Psalm xliv. [22].

No man is fit to comprehend things Heavenly, unless he submit himself to the bearing of adversities for Christ's sake.

Nothing is more acceptable to God, nothing more wholesome to thee in this world, than to suffer cheerfully for Christ.

And if thou couldest choose, thou oughtest rather to wish to suffer adversities for Christ, than to be refreshed with many consolations; because thou wouldest thus be more like unto Christ, and more conformable to all the Saints.

For our worthiness, and the proficiency of our spiritual estate consisteth not in many sweetnesses and comforts; but rather in thoroughly enduring great afflictions and tribulations.

XV. Indeed if there had been any better thing, and more profitable to man's salvation, than suffering, surely Christ would have shewed it by word and example.

For both the disciples that followed Him, and also all who desire to follow Him, He plainly exhorteth to the bearing of the Cross, and saith, 'If any will come after Me, let him deny himself, and take up his Cross, and follow Me.'[1]

So that when we have thoroughly read and searched all, let this be the final conclusion, 'That through many tribulations we must enter into the kingdom of God.'[2]

[1] Luke ix. [23].   [2] Acts xiv. [22].

THE THIRD BOOK

OF INTERNAL CONSOLATION

CHAPTER I

OF CHRIST'S SPEAKING INWARDLY TO THE FAITHFUL SOUL

'I WILL hearken what the Lord God will speak in me.'[1]

Blessed is the soul which heareth the Lord speaking within her,[2] and receiveth from His mouth the word of consolation.

Blessed are the ears that gladly receive the pulses of the Divine whisper,[3] and give no heed to the many whisperings of this world.

Blessed indeed are those ears which listen not after the voice which is sounding without, but for the Truth teaching inwardly.

Blessed are the eyes which are shut to outward things, but intent on things eternal.

Blessed are they that enter far into inward things, and endeavour to prepare themselves more and more, by daily exercises, for the receiving of Heavenly secrets.

Blessed are they who are glad to have time to spare for God, and shake off all worldly impediments.

II. Consider these things, O my soul, and shut up the door of thy sensual desires, that thou mayest hear what the Lord thy God shall speak in thee.[4]

Thus saith thy Beloved, I am thy Salvation,[5] thy

---

[1] Psalm lxxxv. [8]. [2] 1 Sam. ii. [9].
[3] Matt. xiii. [16, 17]. [4] Psalm lxxxv. [8].
[5] Psalm xxxv. [3].

Peace, and thy Life : keep thyself with Me, and thou shalt find peace.

Let go all transitory things, and seek those that be everlasting.

What are all temporal things but seducing snares ? and what can all creatures avail thee, if thou be forsaken by the Creator ?

Bid farewell therefore to all things else, and labour to please thy Creator, and to be faithful unto Him, that so thou mayest be able to attain unto true blessedness.

CHAPTER II

THAT THE TRUTH SPEAKETH INWARDLY WITHOUT NOISE OF WORDS

SPEAK, O Lord, for Thy servant heareth.[1]

I am Thy servant, grant me understanding, that I may know Thy testimonies.[2]

Incline my heart to the words of Thy mouth : let Thy speech distil as the dew.

The children of Israel in times past said unto Moses, 'Speak thou unto us, and we will hear : let not the Lord speak unto us, lest we die.'[3]

Not so, Lord, not so, I beseech Thee : but rather with the prophet Samuel, I humbly and earnestly entreat, 'Speak, Lord, for Thy servant heareth.'

Let not Moses speak unto me, nor any of the prophets, but rather do Thou speak, O Lord God, Inspirer and Enlightener of all the Prophets ; for Thou alone, without them canst perfectly instruct me, but they without Thee can profit nothing.

II. They indeed may sound forth words, but they cannot give the Spirit.

Most beautifully do they speak, but if Thou be silent, they inflame not the heart.

[1] Sam. iii. [9].   [2] Psalm cxix. [125].
[3] Exod. xx. [19].

They teach the letter, but Thou openest the sense : they bring forth mysteries, but Thou unlockest the meaning of sealed things.

They declare Thy commandments, but Thou helpest us to fulfil them.

They point out the way, but Thou givest strength to walk in it.

What they can do is only without, but Thou instructest and enlightenest the heart.

They water outwardly, but Thou givest fruitfulness.

They cry aloud in words, but Thou impartest understanding to the hearing.

III. Let not Moses therefore speak unto me, but Thou, O Lord my God, the Everlasting Truth ; lest I die, and prove unfruitful, if I be only warned outwardly, and not inflamed within.

Lest it turn to my condemnation,—the word heard and not fulfilled, known and not loved, believed and not observed.

Speak therefore, Lord, for Thy servant heareth : for Thou hast the words of eternal life.[1]

Speak Thou unto me, to the comfort, however imperfect, of my soul, and to the amendment of my whole life, and to Thy praise and glory and honour everlasting.

CHAPTER III

THAT THE WORDS OF GOD ARE TO BE HEARD WITH HUMILITY, AND THAT MANY WEIGH THEM NOT

My son, hear My words, words of greatest sweetness, surpassing all the knowledge of the philosophers and wise men of this world. 'My words are Spirit and Life,'[2] and not to be weighed by the understanding of man.

They are not to be drawn forth for vain approbation,

[1] John vi. [68].   [2] John vi. [63].

but to be heard in silence, and to be received with all humility and great affection.

And I said, Blessed is the man whom Thou shalt instruct, O Lord, and shalt teach out of Thy Law, that Thou mayest give him rest from the evil days,[1] and that he be not desolate upon earth.

II. I TAUGHT the Prophets from the beginning,[2] (saith the Lord,) and cease not, even to this day, to speak to all ; but many are hardened, and deaf to My voice.

The generality of persons do more willingly listen to the world than to God ; they sooner follow the desires of their own flesh, than God's good pleasure.

The world promiseth things temporal and mean, and is served with great eagerness : I promise things most high and eternal, and yet the hearts of men remain torpid and insensible.

Who is there that in all things serveth and obeyeth Me with so great care as the world and its lords are served withal ? 'Be ashamed, O Sidon, saith the sea.'[3] And if thou ask the cause, hear wherefore.

For a small income, a long journey is undertaken ; for everlasting life, many will scarce once lift a foot from the ground.

The most pitiful reward is sought after ; for a single bit of money sometimes there is shameful contention ; for a vain matter and slight promise, men fear not to toil day and night.

III. But, alas ! for an unchangeable good, for an inestimable reward, for the highest honour, and glory without end, they grudge even the least fatigue.

Be ashamed, therefore, thou slothful and complaining servant, that they are found to be more ready to destruction than thou to life.

They rejoice more in vanity than thou dost in the truth.

Sometimes, indeed, they are frustrated of their hope ;

[1] Psalm xciv. [12, 13].   [2] Heb. i. [1].
[3] Isaiab xxiii. [4].

but My promise deceiveth none,[1] nor sendeth him away empty that trusteth in Me.

What I have promised, I will give ; what I have said, I will fulfil ; if only any man remain faithful in My love even to the end.

I am the Rewarder of all good men,[2] and the strong Approver of all who are devoted to Me.

IV. Write thou My words in thy heart, and meditate diligently on them ; for in time of temptation they will be very needful for thee.

What thou understandest not when thou readest, thou shalt know in the day of visitation.

In two several ways, I am wont to visit Mine elect, namely with temptation and with consolation.

And I daily read two lessons to them, one in reproving their vices, another in exhorting them to the increase of all virtues.

He that hath My words and despiseth them, hath One that shall judge him in the last day.

V. A Prayer to implore the grace of Devotion.

O Lord my God ! Thou art to me whatsoever is good. And who am I, that I should dare speak to Thee ?[3] I am Thy poorest meanest servant, and a most vile worm, much more poor and contemptible than I can or dare express.

Yet do Thou remember me, O Lord, because I am nothing, I have nothing, and I can do nothing.

Thou alone art Good, Just, and Holy ; Thou canst do all things, Thou accomplishest all things, Thou fillest all things, only the sinner Thou leavest empty.

Remember Thy mercies, and fill my heart with Thy grace, Thou who wilt not that Thy works should be void and in vain.

VI. How can I bear up myself in this miserable life, unless Thou strengthen me with Thy mercy and grace?

[1] Rom. i. [16] ; Matt. xxiv. [35].
[2] Rev. ii. [23] ; Matt. v. [6] ; xxv. [21].
[3] Gen. xviii. [27] ; 1 Sam. xviii. [18, 23].

Turn not Thy face away from me;[1] delay not Thy visitation; withdraw not Thy consolation, lest my soul become as a thirsty land unto Thee.

Teach me, O Lord, to do Thy will;[2] teach me to live worthily and humbly in Thy sight; for Thou art my Wisdom, Thou dost truly know me, and didst know me before the world was made, and before I was born in the world.

CHAPTER IV

THAT WE OUGHT TO LIVE IN TRUTH AND HUMILITY BEFORE GOD

My son, walk thou before Me in truth, and ever seek Me in simplicity of thy heart.[3]

He that walketh before Me in truth, shall be defended from evil incursions, and the Truth shall set him free[4] from seducers, and from the slanders of unjust men.

If the Truth shall have made thee free, thou shalt be free indeed, and shalt not care for the vain words of men.

O Lord, it is true. According as Thou sayest, so, I beseech Thee, let it be with me; let Thy Truth teach me, guard me, and preserve me safe to the end.

Let it set me free from all evil affection and inordinate love; and I shall walk with Thee in great liberty of heart.

II. I WILL teach thee (saith the Truth) those things which are right and pleasing in My sight.

Reflect on thy sins with great displeasure and grief; and never esteem thyself to be any thing, because of any good works.

In truth thou art a sinner; thou art subject to and encumbered with many passions. Of thyself thou

---

[1] Psalm lxix. [17].   [2] Psalm cxliii. [10].
[3] Gen. xvii. [1]; Wisd. i. [1].   [4] John viii. [32].

always tendest to nothing; speedily art thou cast down, speedily overcome, speedily disordered, speedily dissolved.

Thou hast nothing whereof thou canst glory,[1] but many things for which thou oughtest to account thyself vile; for thou art much weaker than thou art able to comprehend.

III. And therefore let nothing seem much unto thee, whatsoever thou doest.

Let nothing seem great, nothing precious and wonderful, nothing worthy of estimation, nothing high, nothing truly commendable and to be desired, but that alone which is eternal.

Let the eternal Truth be above all things pleasing to thee. Let thy own extreme unworthiness be always displeasing to thee.

Fear nothing, blame nothing, flee nothing, so much as thy vices and sins; which ought to be more unpleasing to thee than any losses whatsoever of things earthly.

Some walk not sincerely in My sight,[2] but led by a certain curiosity and pride wish to know My secrets, and to understand the high things of God, neglecting themselves and their own salvation.

These oftentimes, when I resist them, for their pride and curiosity do fall into great temptations and sins.

IV. Fear thou the judgments of God, and dread the wrath of the Almighty. Do not however discuss the works of the Most High, but search diligently thine own iniquities, in how great things thou hast offended, and how many good things thou hast neglected.

Some carry their devotion only in books, some in pictures, some in outward signs and figures.

Some have Me in their mouths, but little in their hearts.[3]

Others there are who, being illuminated in their

[1] 1 Cor. iv. [7].
[2] Ecclus. iii. [21—23]; 2 Cor. ii. [17].
[3] Isaiah xxix. [13].

understandings, and purged in their affection, do always breathe after things eternal, are unwilling to hear of the things of this world, and do serve the necessities of nature with grief ; and these perceive what the Spirit of Truth speaketh in them.[1]

For He teacheth them to despise earthly, and to love heavenly things, to neglect the world, and to desire Heaven all the day and night.[2]

CHAPTER · V

OF THE WONDERFUL EFFECT OF DIVINE LOVE.

I BLESS Thee, O Heavenly Father, Father of my Lord JESUS Christ, for that Thou hast vouchsafed to remember me a poor creature.

O Father of mercies and God of all comfort,[3] thanks be unto Thee, who sometimes with Thy comfort refreshest me, unworthy as I am of all comfort.

I will alway bless and glorify Thee, with Thy only-begotten Son, and the Holy Ghost, the Comforter, for ever and ever.

Ah, Lord God, Thou Holy Lover of my soul, when Thou comest into my heart, all that is within me shall rejoice.

Thou art my Glory and the exultation of my heart : Thou art my Hope and Refuge in the day of my trouble.[4]

II. But because I am as yet weak in love, and imperfect in virtue, I have need to be strengthened and comforted by Thee ; visit me therefore often, and instruct me with all holy discipline.

Set me free from evil passions, and heal my heart of all inordinate affections ; that being inwardly cured and thoroughly cleansed, I may be made fit to love, courageous to suffer steady to persevere.

---

[1] Psalm xxv. [5].   [2] Psalm i. [2].
[3] 2 Cor. i. [3].   [4] Psalm xxxii. [7], lix. [16].

III. Love is a great thing, yea, a great and thorough good ; by itself it makes every thing that is heavy, light ; and it bears evenly all that is uneven.

For it carries a burden which is no burden,[1] and makes every thing that is bitter, sweet and tasteful.

The noble love of JESUS impels a man to do great things, and stirs him up to be always longing for what is more perfect.

Love desires to be aloft, and will not be kept back by any thing low and mean.

Love desires to be free, and estranged from all worldly affections, that so its inward sight may not be hindered ; that it may not be entangled by any temporal prosperity, or by any adversity subdued.

Nothing is sweeter than Love, nothing more courageous, nothing higher, nothing wider, nothing more pleasant, nothing fuller nor better in Heaven and earth ; because Love is born of God, and cannot rest but in God, above all created things.

IV. He that loveth, flyeth, runneth, and rejoiceth ; he is free, and cannot be held in.

He giveth all for all, and hath all in all ; because he resteth in One Highest above all things, from whom all that is good flows and proceeds.

He respecteth not the gifts, but turneth himself above all goods unto the Giver.

Love oftentimes knoweth no measure, but is fervent beyond all measure.

Love feels no burden, thinks nothing of trouble, attempts what is above its strength, pleads no excuse of impossibility ; for it thinks all things lawful for itself and all things possible.

It is therefore able to undertake all things, and it completes many things, and warrants them to take effect, where he who does not love, would faint and lie down.

V. Love is watchful, and sleeping slumbereth not.[2]

Though weary, it is not tired ; though pressed, it is not straitened ; though alarmed, it is not confounded :

---

[1] Matt. xi. [30].   [2] Rom. viii. [19].

but as a lively flame and burning torch, it forces its way upwards, and securely passes through all.

If any man love, he knoweth what is the cry of this voice. For it is a loud cry in the ears of God, the mere ardent affection of the soul, when it saith, 'My God, my Love, Thou art all mine, and I am all Thine.'

VI. Enlarge Thou me in love, that with the inward palate of my heart I may taste how sweet it is to love, and to be dissolved, and as it were to bathe myself in Thy Love.

Let me be possessed by Love, mounting above myself, through excessive fervour and admiration.

Let me sing the song of love, let me follow Thee, my Beloved, on high; let my soul spend itself in Thy praise, rejoicing through love.

Let me love Thee more than myself, nor love myself but for Thee: and in Thee all that truly love Thee, as the law of Love commandeth, shining out from Thyself.

VII. Love is active, sincere, affectionate, pleasant and amiable; courageous, patient, faithful, prudent, long-suffering, manly, and never seeking itself.[1]

For in whatever instance a person seeketh himself, there he falleth from Love.[2]

Love is circumspect, humble, and upright: not yielding to softness, or to levity, nor attending to vain things; it is sober, chaste, steady, quiet, and guarded in all the senses.

Love is subject, and obedient to its superiors, to itself mean and despised, unto God devout and thankful, trusting and hoping always in Him, even then when God imparteth no relish of sweetness unto it: for without sorrow none liveth in love.

VIII. He that is not prepared to suffer all things, and to stand to the will of his Beloved, is not worthy to be called a lover [of God].[3]

A lover ought to embrace willingly all that is hard and distasteful, for the sake of his Beloved; and not to turn away from Him for any contrary accidents.

[1] 1 Cor. xiii. [5].   [2] 1 Cor. x. [33]; Phil. ii. [21].
[3] Rom. viii. [35].

CHAPTER VI

OF THE PROOF OF A TRUE LOVER [OF CHRIST]

My son, thou art not yet a courageous and considerate lover.

WHEREFORE sayest Thou this, O Lord?

BECAUSE for a slight opposition thou givest over thy undertakings, and too eagerly seekest consolation.

A courageous lover standeth firm in temptations, and giveth no credit to the crafty persuasions of the Enemy. As I please him in prosperity, so in adversity I am not unpleasant to him.[1]

II. A considerate lover regardeth not so much the gift of Him who loves him, as the love of the Giver.

He esteems the good will rather than the value [of the gift], and sets all gifts below Him whom he loves.

A noble-minded lover resteth not in the gift, but in Me above every gift.

All therefore is not lost, if sometimes thou hast less feeling for Me or My saints than thou wouldest.

That good and sweet affection which thou sometimes feelest, is the effect of grace present, and a sort of foretaste of thy Heavenly home: but hereon thou must not lean too much, for it comes and goes.

But to strive against evil motions of the mind which may befall thee, and to reject[2] with scorn the suggestions of the devil, is a notable sign of virtue, and shall have great reward.

III. Let no strange fancies therefore trouble thee, which on any subject whatever may crowd into thy mind. Keep to thy purpose, with courage, and an upright intention towards God.

Neither is it an illusion that sometimes thou art suddenly rapt on high, and presently returnest again unto the accustomed vanities of thy heart.

For these thou dost rather unwillingly suffer, than

---

[1] Phil. iv. [11—13].   [2] Matt. iv. [10].

commit : and so long as they displease thee, and thou strivest against them, it is matter of reward, and no loss.

IV. Know that the ancient Enemy doth strive by all means to hinder thy desire to good, and to keep thee clear of all religious exercises ; particularly from the reverend estimation of God's saints, from the devout commemoration of My Passion, from the profitable remembrance of sins, from the guard of thine own heart. and from the firm purpose of advancing in virtue.

Many evil thoughts does he suggest to thee, that so he may cause a wearisomeness and horror in thee, to call thee back from prayer and holy reading.

Humble confession is displeasing unto him ; and if he could, he would cause thee to cease from Holy Communion.

Trust him not, nor care for him, although he should often set snares of deceit to entrap thee.

Charge him with it, when he suggesteth evil and unclean thoughts unto thee ; say unto him,

'Away thou unclean Spirit ! [1] blush, thou miserable wretch ! most unclean art thou that bringest such things unto mine ears.

'Begone from me, thou wicked Seducer ! thou shalt have no part in me : but Jesus shall be with me as a strong Warrior, and thou shalt stand confounded.

'I had rather die, and undergo any torment, than consent unto thee.

'Hold thy peace and be silent ; I will hear thee no more, though thou shouldest work me many troubles. "The Lord is my Light and my Salvation, whom shall I fear ?" [2]

'If whole armies should stand together against me, my heart shall not fear. The Lord is my Helper and my Redeemer.'

V. Fight like a good soldier : [3] and if thou sometimes fall through frailty, take again greater strength

[1] Matt. iv. [10], xvi. [23].   [2] Psalm xxvii. [1].
[3] Psalm xxvii. [14] ; 1 Tim. vi. [12].

than before, trusting in My more abundant Grace : and take great heed of vain pleasing of thyself, and of pride.

This brings many into error, and makes them sometimes fall into blindness almost incurable.

Let the fall of the proud, thus foolishly presuming of themselves, serve thee for a warning and keep thee ever humble.

CHAPTER VII

OF CONCEALING GRACE UNDER THE GUARD OF HUMILITY

My son, it is more profitable for thee and more safe, to conceal the grace of devotion ; not to lift thyself on high, nor to speak much thereof, or to dwell much thereon ; but rather to despise thyself, and to fear it, as given to one unworthy of it.

This affection must not be too earnestly cleaved unto, for it may be quickly changed to the contrary.

Think when thou art in Grace, how miserable and needy thou art wont to be without Grace.

Nor is it in this only that thy progress in spiritual life consists, when thou hast the grace of comfort ; but rather when with humility, self-denial, and patience, thou endurest the withdrawing thereof ; provided thou do not then become listless in the exercise of prayer, nor suffer the rest of thy accustomed duties to be at all neglected.

Rather do thou cheerfully perform what lieth in thee, according to the best of thy power and understanding ; and do not wholly neglect thyself because of the dryness or anxiety of mind which thou feelest.

II. For there are many who when things succeed not well with them, presently become impatient or slothful.

For the way of man is not always in his power,[1] but it belongeth unto God to give, and to comfort, when

---
[1] Jer. x. [23] ; Rom. ix. [16].

He will, and how much He will, and whom He will; as it shall please Him, and no more.

Some unadvised persons, in their over-earnest desire of the grace of a devoted life, have overthrown themselves; because they attempted more than they were able to perform, not weighing the measure of their own weakness, but rather following the desire of their heart, than the judgment of their reason.

And because they presumed on greater matters than was pleasing to God, they therefore quickly·lost His grace.

They who had built themselves nests[1] in Heaven were made helpless and vile outcasts; to the end that being humbled and impoverished, they might learn not to fly with their own wings, but to trust under My feathers.

They that are yet but novices and inexperienced in the way of the Lord, unless they govern themselves by the counsel of discreet persons, may easily be deceived and broken to pieces.

III. And if they will rather follow their own notions than trust to others who are more experienced, their end will be dangerous, at least if they are unwilling to be drawn away from their own fond conceit.

It is seldom the case that they who are self-wise endure humbly to be governed by others.

Better it is to have a small portion of good sense with humility,[2] and a slender understanding, than great treasures of science with vain self-complacency.

Better it is for thee to have little than much of that which may make thee proud.

He acts not very discreetly, who wholly gives himself over to joy, forgetting his former helplessness, and that chastened fear of the Lord, which is afraid of losing the grace which hath been offered.

Nor again is he very valiantly wise who in time of adversity or any heaviness, at once yields too much to despairing thoughts, and reflects, and thinks of Me less confidingly than he ought.

[1] Isaiah xiv. [13].   [2] Psalm xvi. [2], xvii. [10].

IV. He who in time of peace is willing to be over secure,[1] shall be often found in time of war too much dejected and full of fears.

If thou hadst the wit always to continue humble and moderate within thyself, and also thoroughly to moderate and govern thy spirit, thou wouldest not so quickly fall into danger and offence.

It is good counsel, that when fervour of spirit is kindled within thee, thou shouldest consider how it will be, when that light shall leave thee.

And when this does happen, then remember that the light may return again, which as a warning to thyself and for Mine own glory, I have withdrawn for a time.[2]

V. Such trials are oftentimes more profitable, than if thou shouldest always have things prosper according to thy will.

For a man's worthiness is not to be estimated by the number of visions and comforts which he may have, or by his skill in the Scriptures, or by his being placed in a higher station [than others].

But [the proof is] if he be grounded in true humility, and full of divine charity; if he be always purely and sincerely seeking God's honour; if he think nothing of and unfeignedly despise himself,[3] and even rejoice more to be despised and put low by others, than to be honoured by them.

CHAPTER VIII

OF A MEAN CONCEIT OF OURSELVES IN THE SIGHT OF GOD

SHALL I speak unto my Lord, since I am but dust and ashes?[4] If I esteem myself to be any thing more, behold, Thou standest against me, and my iniquities bear true witness, and I cannot contradict it.

---

[1] 1 Thess. v. [6].　　　[2] Job vii.
[3] Psalm lxxxiv. [10].　　[4] Gen. xviii. [27].

But if I abase myself, and reduce myself to nothing, and shrink from all self-esteem, and grind myself to (what I am) dust, Thy grace will be favourable to me, and Thy light near unto my heart; and all self-esteem, how little soever, shall be swallowed up in the valley of my nothingness, and perish for ever.

There Thou shewest Thyself unto me, what I am, what I have been, and whither I am come; for I am nothing, and I knew it not.

If I be left to myself, behold! I become nothing but mere weakness; but if Thou for an instant look upon me, I am forthwith made strong, and am filled with new joy.

And a great marvel it is, that I am so suddenly lifted up, and so graciously embraced by Thee, who of mine own weight am always sinking downward.

II. Thy love is the cause hereof, freely preventing me, and relieving me in so many necessities, guarding me also from pressing dangers, and snatching me (as I may truly say), from evils out of number.

For indeed by loving myself amiss, I lost myself;[1] and by seeking Thee alone, and purely loving Thee, I have found both myself and Thee, and by that love have more deeply reduced myself to nothing.

Because Thou, O sweetest Lord, dealest with me above all desert, and above all that I dare hope for or ask.

III. Blessed be Thou, my God: for although I be unworthy of any benefits, yet Thy noble bounty and infinite goodness never ceaseth to do good even to the ungrateful,[2] and to those who are turned away far from Thee.

Turn Thou us unto Thee, that we may be thankful, humble, and devout; for Thou art our salvation, our courage, and our strength.

[1] John xii. [25].   [2] Matt. v. [45].

CHAPTER IX

THAT ALL THINGS ARE TO BE REFERRED UNTO GOD, AS THEIR LAST END

My son, I ought to be thy supreme and ultimate end, if thou desire to be truly blessed.

With this intention thy affections will be purified, which are too often inordinately inclined to selfishness and unto creatures.

For if in any thing thou seekest thyself, immediately thou faintest and driest up.

I would therefore thou shouldest refer all things principally unto Me, for I am He who have given all.

Consider every thing as flowing from the Highest Good ;[1] and therefore unto Me as their Original all must be reduced.

II. From Me, as from a living fountain, the small and the great, the poor and the rich, do draw the water of life ;[2] and they that willingly and freely serve Me, shall receive grace for grace.

But he who desires to glory in things out of Me,[3] or to take pleasure in some private good, shall not be grounded in true joy, nor be enlarged in his heart, but shall many ways be encumbered and straitened.

Thou oughtest therefore to ascribe nothing of good to thyself, nor do thou attribute goodness unto any man ; but give all unto God, without whom man hath nothing.

I have bestowed all,[4] and My will is to have thee all again ; and with great strictness do I require a return of thanks.

III. This is the truth whereby vain-glory is put to flight.

And if Heavenly grace enter in and true charity, there will be no envy nor narrowness of heart, neither will self-love busy itself.

[1] Ecclus. i. [5].   [2] John iv. [14].
[3] 1 Cor. i. [20].   [4] 1 Cor. iv. [7].

For Divine charity overcometh all things, and enlargeth all the powers of the soul.

If thou rightly judge, thou wilt rejoice in Me alone, in Me alone thou wilt hope ; for none is good save God alone,[1] who is to be praised above all things, and in all to be blessed.

CHAPTER X

THAT TO DESPISE THE WORLD AND SERVE GOD IS A SWEET LIFE

Now I will speak again, O Lord, and will not be silent ; I will say in the ears of my God, my Lord, and my King, who is on high : 'O how great is the abundance of Thy goodness, O Lord, which Thou hast laid up for them that fear Thee.'[2]

But what art Thou to those who love Thee ? what to those who serve Thee with their whole heart ?

Truly unspeakable is the sweetness of contemplating Thee, which Thou bestowest on them that love Thee.

In this especially Thou hast shewed me the sweetness of Thy charity ; that when I was not, Thou madest me, when I went far astray from Thee, Thou broughtest me back again, that I might serve Thee, and hast commanded me to love Thee.[3]

II. O Fountain of love unceasing, what shall I say concerning Thee ?

How can I forget Thee, who hast vouchsafed to remember me, even after I had wasted away and perished ?

Thou hast shewed mercy to Thy servant beyond all expectation ; and hast exhibited favour and loving-kindness beyond all desert.

[1] Matt. xix. [17] ; Luke xviii. [19].
[2] Psalm xxxi. [19].
[3] Gen. i. [27] ; Psalm cxix. [73] ; Matt. xv. [perhaps x. 37].

What return shall I make to Thee for this grace?[1]

For it is not granted to all to forsake all, to renounce the world, and to undertake a life of religious retiredness.

Is it any great thing that I should serve Thee,[2] whom the whole creation is bound to serve?

It ought not to seem much to me, to serve Thee ; but rather this doth appear much to me, and wonderful, that Thou vouchsafest to receive into Thy service, one so poor and unworthy, and to make him one with Thy beloved servants.

III. Behold ! all things are Thine which I have, and whereby I serve Thee.[3]

And yet contrariwise, Thou rather servest me than I Thee.

Behold ! heaven and earth, which Thou hast created for the service of man, are ready at hand, and do daily perform whatever Thou hast commanded.

And this is little ; Thou hast moreover also appointed Angels to minister to man.[4]

But that which excelleth all this is, that Thou Thyself hast vouchsafed to serve man, and hast promised that Thou wouldest give Thyself unto him.

IV. What shall I give Thee for all these thousands of benefits? I would I could serve Thee all the days of my life.

I would I were able, at least for one day, to do Thee some worthy service.

Truly Thou art worthy of all service, of all honour and everlasting praise.

Truly Thou art my Lord, and I Thy poor servant, who am bound to serve Thee with all my might, neither ought I ever to be weary of praising Thee.

And this I wish to do, this I desire ; and whatsoever is wanting unto me, do Thou, I beseech Thee, vouchsafe to supply.

V. It is a great honour, and a great glory, to serve Thee, and despise all things for Thee.

[1] Psalm cxvi. [12].   [2] Judges xvi. [15].
[3] 1 Cor. iv. [7].   [4] Psalm xci. [11] ; Heb. i. [14].

For great grace shall be given to those who shall have willingly subjected themselves to Thy most holy service.

They who for Thy love shall have renounced all carnal delights, shall find the sweetest consolations of the Holy Ghost.[1]

They shall attain great freedom of mind, who for Thy Name's sake enter into the narrow way,[2] and have left off all worldly care.

VI. O sweet and delightful service of God,[3] by which a man is made truly free and holy !

O sacred state of religious servitude, which makes a man equal to the Angels, pleasing to God, terrible to devils, and worthy to be commended of all the faithful.

O welcome service and ever to be desired, in which we are rewarded with the Greatest Good and attain to joy which shall endlessly remain with us !

CHAPTER XI

THAT THE LONGINGS AND DESIRES OF OUR HEARTS ARE TO BE EXAMINED AND MODERATED.

My son, it is needful for thee still to learn many things more, which thou hast not even yet well learned.

What are these, O Lord ?

That thou frame thy desires [4] wholly according to My good pleasure ; and that thou be not a lover of thyself, but an earnest follower of My will.

Various longings and desires oftentimes inflame thee, and drive thee forwards with vehemence ; but do thou consider whether thou be not moved rather for thine own advantage, than for My honour.

If I Myself be the cause, thou wilt be well content with whatsoever I shall ordain ; but if there lurk in

[1] Matt. xix..[29].   [2] Matt. vii. [14].
[3] Matt. xi. [30] ; 1 John v. [3].
[4] Psalm cviii. [1] ; Matt. vi. [10].

thee any self-seeking,[1] behold, this it is that hindereth thee and weigheth thee down.

II. Beware therefore thou lean not too much upon any preconceived desire, without asking My counsel, lest perhaps afterwards it repent thee, or thou be displeased with that which at first pleased thee, and which thou wast earnestly zealous for, as being the best.

For not every affection which seems good is immediately to be followed ; nor again is every contrary affection at the first to be avoided.

It is sometimes expedient to use a restraint even in good desires and endeavours, lest through importunity thou incur distraction of mind ; lest by thy want of self-government thou beget a scandal unto others ; or again being by others thwarted and resisted thou become suddenly confounded, and so fall.

III. Sometimes however thou must use violence,[2] and resist manfully thy sensual appetite, not regarding what the flesh would, or would not ;[3] but rather taking pains that even perforce it may be made subject to the Spirit.[4]

And so long ought it to be chastised and to be forced to remain under servitude, until it be prepared for every thing, and learn to be content with a little, and to be pleased with plain and simple things, nor to murmur against any inconvenience.

CHAPTER XII

OF THE GROWTH OF PATIENCE IN THE SOUL, AND OF STRIVING AGAINST CONCUPISCENCE

O LORD my God, patience is very necessary for me,[5] as I see that many things in this life do happen as we would not.

[1] Phil. ii. [21]. [2] Phil. ii. [12].
[3] Rom. viii. [1—13] ; 2 Cor. iv. [10], x. [3].
[4] 1 Cor. ix. [27]. [5] Heb. x. [36].

For whatever plans I shall devise for my own peace, my life cannot be without war and affliction.[1]

IT is so, My son. But My will is, that thou seek not that peace which is void of temptation, or which feeleth nothing contrary; but rather think that thou hast then found peace, when thou art exercised with sundry tribulations,[2] and tried in many adversities.

II. If thou say, that thou art not able to suffer much, how then wilt thou endure the fire hereafter?

Of two evils the less is always to be chosen.

That thou mayest therefore avoid the future everlasting punishment, endeavour to endure present evils patiently for God's sake.

Dost thou think that the men of this world suffer nothing or but a little? Ask even of those who enjoy the greatest delicacies, and thou shalt find it otherwise.

But thou wilt say, they have many delights, and follow their own wills, and therefore they do not much weigh their own afflictions.

Be it so, that they do have whatsoever they will; but how long dost thou think it will last?

III. Behold, the wealthy of this world shall consume away like smoke,[3] and there shall be no memory of their past joys!

Yea, even while they are yet alive, they do not rest in them without bitterness, weariness, and fear.

For from the self-same thing in which they imagine their delight to be, oftentimes they receive the penalty of sorrow.

Nor is it any thing but just, that having inordinately sought and followed after pleasures, they should enjoy them not without shame and bitterness.

IV. O how brief, how false, how inordinate and filthy, are all those pleasures.

Yet so drunken and blind are men that they understand it not; but like dumb beasts, for the poor enjoyment of this corruptible life, they incur the death of the soul.

[1] Job vii. [1]. [2] James i. [2]. [3] Psalm lxviii. [2].

Thou therefore, My son, 'go not after thy lusts, but refrain thyself from thine appetites.'[1] 'Delight thyself in the LORD, and He shall give thee the desires of thine heart.'[2]

V. For if thou desire true delight, and to be more plentifully comforted by Me; behold, in the contempt of all worldly things, and in the cutting off all base delights, shall be thy blessing, and abundant consolation shall be rendered to thee.

And the more thou withdrawest thyself from all solace of creatures, so much the sweeter and more powerful consolations shalt thou find in Me.

But at the first, thou shalt not without some sadness, nor without a laborious conflict, attain unto these consolations.

Old inbred habits will make resistance, but by better habits they shall be entirely overcome.

The flesh will murmur against thee; but with fervency of spirit thou shalt bridle it.

The Old Serpent will instigate and trouble thee, but by prayer he shall be put to flight; moreover also, by any useful employment thou shalt greatly stop the way against him.

CHAPTER XIII

OF THE OBEDIENCE OF ONE IN HUMBLE SUBJECTION, AFTER THE EXAMPLE OF JESUS CHRIST

My son, he that endeavoureth to withdraw himself from obedience, withdraweth himself from Grace: and he who seeketh for himself private benefits[3] loseth those which are common.

He that doth not cheerfully and freely submit himself to his superior, it is a sign that his flesh is not as

[1] Ecclus. xviii. [30].   [2] Psalm xxxvii. [4].
[3] Matt. xvi. [24].

yet perfectly obedient unto him, but oftentimes kicketh and murmureth against him.

Learn thou therefore quickly to submit thyself to thy superior, if thou desire to keep thine own flesh under the yoke.

For more speedily is the outward enemy overcome, if the inward man be not laid waste.

There is no worse enemy, nor one more troublesome to the soul, than thou art unto thyself, if thou be not well in harmony with the Spirit.

It is altogether necessary that thou take up a true contempt for thyself, if thou desire to prevail against flesh and blood.

II. Because as yet thou lovest thyself too inordinately, therefore thou art afraid to resign thyself wholly to the will of others.

And yet, what great matter is it, if thou, who art but dust and nothing, subject thyself to a man for God's sake, when I, the Almighty and the Most Highest, who created all things of nothing, humbly subjected Myself to man for thy sake?

I became of all men the most humble and the most abject,[1] that thou mightest overcome thy pride with My humility.

O dust, learn to be obedient. Learn to humble thyself, thou earth and clay, and to bow thyself down under the feet of all men.

Learn to break thine own wishes, and to yield thyself to all subjection.

III Be fiercely hot against thyself, and suffer no pride to dwell in thee : but shew thyself so humble and so very small, that all may be able to walk over thee, and to tread thee down as the mire of the streets. Vain man, what hast thou to complain of?

What canst thou answer, foul sinner, to them that upbraid thee, thou who hast so often offended God; and so many times deserved hell?

But Mine eye spared thee, because thy soul was

---

[1] Luke ii. [7]; John xiii. [14].

precious in My sight; that thou mightest know My love, and ever be thankful for My benefits;

Also that thou mightest continually give thyself to true subjection and humility, and endure patiently the contempt which belongs to thee.

CHAPTER XIV

OF THE DUTY OF CONSIDERING THE SECRET JUDGMENTS OF GOD, THAT SO WE BE NOT LIFTED UP FOR ANY THING GOOD IN US

THOU, O Lord, thunderest forth Thy judgments over me, Thou shakest all my bones with fear and trembling, and my soul is very sore afraid.

I stand astonished; and I consider 'That the Heavens are not pure in Thy sight.' [1]

If in Angels Thou didst find wickedness,[2] and didst not spare even them, what shall become of me?

Even stars fell from Heaven,[3] what then can I presume who am but dust?

They whose works seemed commendable, have fallen into the lowest misery; and those who did eat the bread of Angels,[4] I have seen delighting themselves with the husks of swine.

II. There is therefore no sanctity, if Thou, O Lord, withdraw Thine hand.

No wisdom availeth, if Thou cease to guide.

No courage helpeth, if Thou leave off to defend.

No chastity is secure, if Thou do not protect it.

No custody of our own availeth, if Thy sacred watchfulness be not present with us.

For, if we be left to ourselves, we sink and perish; but being visited of Thee, we are raised up and live.

Truly we are unstable, but through Thee we are

---

[1] Job xv. [15].   [2] Job iv. [18].
[3] Rev. viii. [10].   [4] Ps. lxxviii. [25].

strengthened: we wax lukewarm, but by Thee we are inflamed.

III. O how humbly and meanly ought I to think of myself! how ought I to esteem it as nothing, if I should seem to have any good quality!

With what profound humility ought I to submit myself to Thy unfathomable judgments, O Lord; where I find myself to be nothing else than Nothing, and [still] Nothing!

O unmeasurable weight! O sea that can never be passed over, where I [can] discover nothing of myself save only and wholly Nothing!

Where then is the lurking-place of glory? where the confidence conceived of virtue?

All vain-glorying is swallowed up in the deep of Thy judgments over me.

IV. What is all flesh in Thy sight?

Shall the clay glory against Him that formeth it?

How can he be lifted up with vain words whose heart is truly subject to God?[1]

Not all the world can lift up him, whom the Truth hath subjected unto itself: neither shall he, who hath firmly settled his whole hope in God, be moved with the tongues of any who praise him.

For even they themselves who speak, behold they all are nothing, for they will pass away with the sound of their own words; but the Truth of the Lord remaineth for ever.[2]

CHAPTER XV

IN EVERY THING WHICH WE DESIRE, HOW WE OUGHT TO STAND AFFECTED, AND WHAT WE OUGHT TO SAY.

My son, say thou thus in every thing: 'Lord, if this ' be pleasing unto Thee, so let it be.[3]

---

[1] Isaiah xxix. [16]; Ecclus. xxiii. [4, 5].
[2] Psalm cxvii. [2].   [3] James iii. [perhaps iv. 15].

'Lord, if it be to Thy honour, in Thy Name let this
'be done.

'Lord, if Thou seest it expedient, and allowest it to
'be profitable for me, then grant unto me that I may
'use this to Thine honour.

'But if Thou knowest it will be hurtful unto me,
'and no profit to the health of my soul, take away any
'such desire from me.'

For every desire proceedeth not from the Holy Spirit,
even though it seem unto a man right and good.

It is difficult to judge truly whether a good Spirit or
the contrary drive thee to desire this or that; or
whether by thine own spirit thou be moved thereunto.

Many have been deceived in the end, who at the
first seemed to be led on by a good Spirit.

II. Therefore whatever occurs to the mind as desirable, must always be desired and prayed for in the fear
of God and with humility of heart; and chiefly thou
must commit the whole matter to Me with special
resignation of thyself, and thou must say,

'O Lord, Thou knowest what is best for us, let this
'or that be done, as Thou shalt please.

'Give what Thou wilt, and how much Thou wilt, and
'when Thou wilt.

'Deal with me as Thou thinkest good, and as best
'pleases Thee, and is most for Thy honour.

'Set me where Thou wilt, and deal with me in all
'things just as Thou wilt.

'I am in Thy hand: turn me round, and turn me
'back again, as Thou shalt please.

'Behold, I am Thy servant, prepared for all things;
'for I desire not to live unto myself, but unto Thee;
'and O that I could do it worthily and perfectly!'

A Prayer that the will of God may be fulfilled.

III. O most merciful Jesus, grant to me Thy Grace,
that it may be with me, and labour with me,[1] and
persevere with me even to the end.

[1] Wisd. ix. [10].

Grant that I may always desire and will that which is to Thee most acceptable, and most dear.

Let Thy will be mine, and let my will ever follow Thine, and agree perfectly with it.

Let my will and nill be all one with Thine, and let me not be able to will or nill any thing else, but what Thou willest or nillest.

IV. Grant that I may die to all things that are in the world, and for Thy sake love to be contemned, and not known in this generation.

Grant to me above all things that can be desired, to rest in Thee, and in Thee to have my heart at peace.

Thou art the true peace of the heart, Thou its only rest; out of Thee all things are hard and restless. In this very peace, that is, in Thee, the one Chiefest Eternal Good, I will sleep and rest.[1] Amen.

CHAPTER XVI

THAT TRUE COMFORT IS TO BE SOUGHT IN GOD ALONE

WHATSOEVER I can desire or imagine for my comfort, I look for it not here but hereafter.

For if I might alone have all the comforts of the world, and were able to enjoy all the delights thereof,[2] it is certain that they could not long endure.

Wherefore, O my soul, thou canst not be fully comforted,[3] nor have perfect refreshment, except in God, the Comforter of the poor, and Patron of the humble.

Wait a little while, O my soul, wait for the Divine promise, and thou shalt have abundance of all good things in Heaven.

If thou desire inordinately the things that are present, thou shalt lose those which are heavenly and eternal.

[1] Psalm iv. [8].   [2] Matt. xvi. [26].
[3] Psalm lxxvii. [1, 2].

Use temporal things, and desire eternal.

Thou canst not be satisfied with any temporal goods, because thou art not created to enjoy them.

11. Although thou shouldest possess all created good, yet couldest thou not be happy thereby nor blessed; but in God, who created all things, consisteth thy whole blessedness and felicity;[1] not such as is seen and commended by the foolish lovers of the world, but such as the good and faithful servants of Christ wait for, and of which the spiritual and pure in heart, whose conversation is in Heaven,[2] sometimes have a foretaste.

Vain and brief is all human consolation.

Blessed and true is the consolation which is received inwardly from the Truth.

A devout man beareth every where about with him his own Comforter Jesus, and saith unto Him, 'Be 'Thou present with me, O Lord Jesu, in every time and 'place.

'Let this be my consolation, to be cheerfully willing 'to do without all human comfort.

'And if Thy consolation be wanting, let Thy will and 'just trial of me be unto me as the greatest comfort; for 'Thou wilt not always be angry, neither wilt Thou 'threaten for ever.'[3]

CHAPTER XVII

THAT ALL OUR ANXIETIES ARE TO BE PLACED ON GOD

My son, suffer me to do with thee what I please, I know what is expedient for thee.

Thou thinkest as man; thou judgest in many things as human feelings persuade thee.

---

[1] Wisd. ii. [23].   [2] Phil. iii. [20].
[3] Ps. ciii. [9].

O LORD, what Thou sayest is true. Thy anxiety for me is greater[1] than all the care that I can take for myself.

For he standeth but very totteringly, who casteth not all his anxiety upon Thee.

O Lord, if only my will may remain right and firm towards Thee, do with me whatsoever it shall please Thee.

For it cannot be any thing but good, whatsoever Thou shalt do with me.

II. If it be Thy will I should be in darkness, be Thou blessed; and if it be Thy will I should be in light, be thou again blessed. If Thou vouchsafe to comfort me, be Thou blessed; and if Thou wilt have me afflicted, be Thou ever equally blessed.

My son, such as this ought to be thy state, if thou desire to walk with Me.

Thou oughtest to be as ready to suffer as to rejoice.

Thou oughtest as cheerfully to be destitute and poor, as full and rich.

III. O LORD, for Thy sake, I will cheerfully suffer[2] whatever shall come on me with Thy permission.

From Thy hand I am willing to receive indifferently good and evil, sweet and bitter, joy and sorrow, and for all that befalleth me I will be thankful.

Keep me safe from all sin, and I shall fear neither death[3] nor hell.

So as Thou dost not cast me from Thee for ever, nor blot me out of the book of life, whatever tribulation may befall me shall not hurt me.

[1] Matt. vi. [30]; John vi. [20].   [2] Job ii. [10].
[3] Ps. xxiii. [4].

CHAPTER XVIII

THAT TEMPORAL MISERIES MUST BE BORNE PATIENTLY, AFTER THE EXAMPLE OF CHRIST

My son, I descended from Heaven [1] for thy salvation; I took upon Me thy miseries,[2] not necessity but charity drawing Me thereto; that thou thyself mightest learn patience, and bear temporal miseries without grudging.

For from the hour of My birth,[3] even until My death on the cross, I was not without suffering of grief.

I suffered great want of things temporal; I often heard many complaints against Me; I endured with benignity disgraces and revilings; in return for benefits I received ingratitude; for miracles, blasphemies; for heavenly doctrine, reproofs.

II. O Lord, for that Thou wert patient in Thy lifetime, herein especially fulfilling the commandment of Thy Father;[4] it is reason that I, a most miserable sinner, should bear myself patiently according to Thy will, and for my soul's welfare endure the burden of this corruptible life as long as Thou Thyself shall choose.

For although this present life be burdensome to our feelings, yet notwithstanding it is now by Thy grace made very gainful; and by Thy example and the footsteps of Thy Saints, more bright and endurable to the weak.

It is, too, much more full of consolation than it was formerly in the old Law, when the gate of Heaven remained shut; and the way also to Heaven seemed more obscure, when so few took care to seek after the kingdom of Heaven.[5]

Moreover also they who then were just and such as should be saved, could not enter into the Heavenly

---

[1] John iii. [13].   [2] Isa. liii. [4].
[3] Luke ii. [7].   [4] John v. [30].
[5] Matt. vii. [14].

kingdom, before Thy Passion, and the due satisfaction of Thy holy death.

III. O how great thanks am I bound to render unto Thee, that Thou hast vouchsafed to shew unto me and to all faithful people the good and the right way to Thine eternal kingdom.

For Thy life is our way, and by holy patience we walk toward Thee, who art our Crown.

If Thou hadst not gone before us and taught us, who would have cared to follow?

Alas, how many would remain behind and afar off, if they considered not Thy most noble example!

Behold, we are even yet lukewarm, though we have heard of so many of Thy miracles and doctrines; what would become of us, if we had not so great Light[1] whereby to follow Thee!

CHAPTER XIX

OF THE ENDURANCE OF INJURIES, AND OF THE PROOF OF TRUE PATIENCE

WHAT is it thou sayest, My son? Cease to complain when thou considerest My Passion, and the sufferings of other holy persons.

Thou hast not yet made resistance unto blood.[2]

It is but little which thou sufferest, in comparison of those who suffered so much, who were so strongly tempted, so grievously afflicted, so many ways tried and exercised.[3]

Thou oughtest therefore to call to mind the more heavy sufferings of others, that so thou mayest the easier bear thy own very small troubles.

And if they seem unto thee not very small, then beware lest thy impatience be the cause thereof.

However, whether they be small or whether they be great, endeavour patiently to undergo them all.

[1] John xii. [46]. [2] Heb. xii. [4].
[3] Heb. xi. [37].

II. The better thou disposest thyself to suffering, so much the more wisely thou doest, and so much the greater reward shalt thou receive ; thou shalt also more easily endure it, if both in mind and by habit thou art diligently prepared thereunto.

Do not say, ' I cannot endure to suffer these things at the hands of such an one, nor ought I to endure things of this sort ; for he hath done me great wrong, and reproacheth me with things which I never thought of ; but of another I will willingly suffer, that is, if they are also things which I shall see I ought to suffer.'

Such a thought is foolish ; it considereth not the virtue of patience, nor by whom it will be to be crowned but rather, weigheth too exactly the persons, and the injuries offered to itself.

III. He is not truly patient, who is willing to suffer only so much as he thinks good, and from whom he pleases.

But the truly patient man minds not by whom he is exercised, whether by his superiors, by one of his equals, or by an inferior ; whether by a good and holy man, or by one that is perverse and unworthy.

But indifferently from every creature, how much soever, or how often soever any thing adverse befals him, he takes it all thankfully as from the hands of God, and esteems it a great gain :

For with God it is impossible that any thing, how small soever, if only it be suffered for God's sake, should pass without its reward.

IV. Be thou therefore prepared for the fight, if thou wilt have the victory.

Without a combat thou canst not attain unto the crown of patience.[1]

If thou art unwilling to suffer, thou refusest to be crowned. But if thou desire to be crowned, fight manfully, endure patiently.

Without labour there is no arriving at rest, nor without fighting can the victory be reached.

[1] 2 Tim. ii. [3—5].

O Lord, let that become possible to me by Thy grace, which by nature seems impossible to me.

Thou knowest that I am able to suffer but little, and that I am quickly cast down, when a slight adversity ariseth.

For Thy Name's sake, let every exercise of tribulation be made amiable and desirable to me; for to suffer and to be disquieted for Thy sake, is very wholesome for my soul.

CHAPTER XX

OF THE ACKNOWLEDGING OF OUR OWN INFIRMITIES; AND OF THE MISERIES OF THIS LIFE

I WILL confess against myself mine own unrighteousness;[1] I will confess my weakness unto Thee, O Lord.

Oftentimes a small matter it is that makes me sad and dejected.

I resolve that I will act with courage, but when even a small temptation comes, I am at once in a great strait.

It is sometimes a very trifle, whence a great temptation arises.

And whilst I am thinking myself tolerably safe, and when I least expect it, I sometimes find myself almost entirely overcome by a slight breath.

II. Behold therefore, O Lord, my low state,[2] and my frailty every way known unto Thee.

Have mercy on me, and deliver me out of the mire, that I may not stick fast therein,[3] may not remain utterly cast down for ever.

This is that which oftentimes strikes me backwards, and confounds me in Thy sight, that I am so subject to fall, and weak in resisting my passions.

---

[1] Psalm xxxii. [5].   [2] Psalm xxv. [18].
[3] Psalm lxix. [14].

And although I do not altogether consent, yet their continued assaults are troublesome and grievous unto me ; and it is very exceedingly irksome to live thus daily in conflict.

From hence my weakness becomes known unto me, in that hateful fancies do always much more easily invade than forsake me.

III. Most mighty God of Israel, Thou zealous Lover of faithful souls ! O that Thou wouldst consider the labour and sorrow of Thy servant, and assist him in all things whatsoever he undertaketh.

Strengthen me with heavenly courage, lest the old man, the miserable flesh, not as yet fully subject to the Spirit, prevail and get the upper hand ; against which, it will be needful for me to fight, as long as I breathe in this miserable life.

Alas, what a kind of life is this, where tribulation and miseries are never wanting ; where all is full of snares, and enemies !

For when one tribulation or temptation retreateth, another cometh on ; yea and while the first conflict is yet lasting, many others come unexpected one after another.

IV. And how can a life be loved that hath so many embitterments, and is subject to so many calamities and miseries ?

How too can it be called a life, that begetteth so many deaths and plagues ?

And yet it is the object of men's love, and many seek to delight themselves therein.

The world is oftentimes blamed for being deceitful and vain, and yet men do not easily part with it, because the desires of the flesh bear so great a sway.

But some things draw us to love the world, others to contemn it.

The lust of the flesh, the lust of the eyes, and the pride of life,[1] do draw us to the love of the world ; but the pains and miseries that do justly follow them cause a hatred of the world and a loathsomeness thereof.

---

[1] 1 John ii. [16].

V. But alas, the fondness for vicious pleasures over-cometh the mind of him who is addicted to the world; and he esteemeth it a delight to be under thorns,[1] because he hath neither seen nor tasted the sweetness of God, and the inward pleasantness of virtue.

But they who perfectly contemn the world, and study to live to God under holy discipline, these are not ignorant of the Divine sweetness promised to those who truly forsake the world; they also very clearly see how grievously the world erreth, and how it is in many ways deceived.

CHAPTER XXI

THAT WE ARE TO REST IN GOD ABOVE ALL THINGS WHICH ARE GOOD, AND ABOVE ALL HIS OWN GIFTS

ABOVE all things, and in all things, O my soul, thou shalt rest in the Lord alway, for He Himself is the everlasting Rest of the Saints.

Grant me, O most sweet and loving JESUS, to rest in Thee above all creatures,[2] above all health and beauty, above all glory and honour, above all power and dignity, above all knowledge and subtilty, above all riches and arts, above all joy and gladness, above all fame and praise, above all sweetness and comfort, above all hope and promise, above all desert and desire:

Above all gifts and favours that Thou canst give and impart unto us, above all mirth and jubilee that the mind of man can receive and feel:

Finally above Angels and Archangels, and above all the Heavenly host, above all things visible and invisible, and above all that Thou art not, O my God.

II. Because Thou, O Lord my God, art supremely good above all; Thou alone art most high, Thou alone most powerful, Thou alone most full and sufficient, Thou alone most sweet and most full of consolation:

[1] Job xxx. [7].   [2] Rom. viii. [19—22].

Thou alone art most lovely and loving, Thou alone most noble and glorious above all things, in whom all good things together both perfectly are, and ever have been, and shall be.

And therefore it is too small, and unsatisfying, whatsoever Thou bestowest on me besides Thyself, or revealest unto me of Thyself, or promisest, whilst Thou art not seen, and not fully obtained.

For surely my heart cannot truly rest, nor be entirely contented, unless it rest in Thee, and surmount all gifts and all creatures whatsoever.

III. O Thou most beloved spouse of my soul, Jesu Christ, Thou most pure Lover, Thou Lord of all creation : O that I had the wings of true liberty, that I might flee away and rest in Thee ! [1]

O when shall it be fully granted me, to consider in quietness of mind and see how sweet Thou art, my Lord God ?

When shall I fully gather up myself into Thee, that by reason of my love to Thee I may not feel myself, but Thee alone, above all sense and measure, in a manner not known unto every one ! [2]

But now I oftentimes sigh, and bear my infelicity with grief.

Because many evils occur in this vale of miseries, which do often trouble, grieve, and overcloud me ; often hinder and distract me, allure and entangle me, so that I can have no free access unto Thee, nor enjoy the sweet welcomings which are ever ready with the blessed spirits.

O let my sighs move Thee, and my manifold desolation here on earth.

IV. O Jesu, Thou brightness of eternal glory, Thou comfort of the pilgrim soul, with Thee is my tongue without voice, and my very silence speaketh unto Thee.

How long doth my Lord delay to come ?

Let Him come unto me His poor despised servant, and let Him make me glad. Let Him put forth His hand, and deliver a poor wretch from all anguish.

[1] Ps. lv. [6].   [2] Dan. x. [11].

Come, O come ; for without Thee I shall have no joyful day nor hour ; for Thou art my joy, and without Thee my table is empty.

A wretched creature am I, and in a manner imprisoned and loaded with fetters, until Thou refresh me with the light of Thy presence, and grant me liberty, and shew a friendly countenance toward me.

V. Let others seek what they please instead of Thee ; but for me, nothing else doth nor shall delight me, but Thou only, my God, my hope, my everlasting salvation.

I will not hold my peace, nor cease to pray, until Thy grace return again, and Thou speak inwardly unto me.

BEHOLD, here I am. Behold, I come unto thee, because thou hast called upon Me. Thy tears and the desire of thy soul, thy humiliation and thy contrition of heart, have inclined and brought Me unto thee.

And I said, LORD, I have called upon Thee, and have desired to enjoy Thee, being ready to refuse all things for Thy sake.

For Thou first hast stirred me up that I might seek Thee.

Blessed be Thou therefore, O Lord, that hast shewed this goodness to Thy servant, according to the multitude of Thy mercies.

VI. What hath Thy servant more to say before Thee ? he can only greatly humble himself in Thy sight, ever mindful of his own iniquity and vileness.

For there is none like unto Thee [1] in all the wonderful things of Heaven and earth.

Thy works are very good, Thy judgments true, and by Thy providence the universe is governed.

Praise therefore and glory be unto Thee, O Wisdom of the Father : let my mouth, my soul, and all creatures together, praise and bless thee.

[1] Psalm lxxxvi. [8].

I

CHAPTER XXII

OF THE REMEMBRANCE OF GOD'S MANIFOLD BENEFITS

OPEN, O Lord, my heart in Thy law, and teach me to walk in Thy commandments.[1]

Grant me to understand Thy will, and with great reverence and diligent consideration to remember Thy benefits, as well in general as in particular, that henceforward I may be able worthily to give Thee thanks.

But I know, and confess, that I am not able, even in the least point, to give Thee due thanks for the favours which Thou bestowest upon me.

I am less than the least of all Thy benefits: and when I consider Thine excellency, the greatness thereof maketh my spirit to faint.

II. All that we have in soul and in body, and whatsoever we possess outwardly or inwardly, naturally or supernaturally, are Thy benefits, and do proclaim Thee bountiful, merciful, and good, from whom we have received all good things.

Although one have received more, another less, all notwithstanding are Thine, and without Thee even the least blessing cannot be had.

He that hath received the greatest cannot glory of his own desert, nor extol himself above others, nor insult over the lesser; for he is the greatest and the best, who ascribeth least unto himself, and who in rendering thanks is the most humble and the most devout.

And he that esteemeth himself viler than all men, and judgeth himself most unworthy, is fittest to receive the greater blessings.

III. But he that hath received fewer, ought not to be out of heart, nor to take it grievously, nor envy them that are enriched with greater store; but rather he should turn his mind to Thee, and exceedingly praise Thy goodness, for that Thou bestowest Thy gifts so

[1] Psalm cxix.

bountifully, so freely, and so willingly, without respect of persons.

All things proceed from Thee, and therefore in all Thou art to be praised.

Thou knowest what is fit to be given to every one; and why this man should have less and that more, it is not for us to judge, but for Thee who dost exactly mark every one's deserts.

IV. Wherefore, O Lord God, I even esteem it a great mercy, not to have much of that which outwardly and in the opinion of men seems worthy of glory and applause. For so it is, that he who considers the poverty and unworthiness of his own person, should be so far from conceiving grief or sadness, or from being cast down thereat, that he rather should take great comfort, and be glad; because Thou, O God, hast chosen the poor and humble and the despised of this world for Thyself,[1] for Thy familiar and domestic attendants.

Witnesses are Thy Apostles themselves, whom Thou hast made princes over all the earth.[2]

And yet they lived in the world without complaint,[3] so humble and simple, without all malice and deceit, that they even rejoiced to suffer reproach for Thy Name;[4] and what the world abhorreth, they embraced with great affection.

V. When therefore a man loveth Thee and acknowledgeth Thy benefits, nothing ought so to rejoice him as Thy will toward him, and the good pleasure of Thine eternal appointment.

And herewith he ought to be so contented and comforted, that he would as willingly be the least, as another would wish to be the greatest.

He would too be as peaceable and contented in the last place as in the first; as willing to be a despised cast-away, of no name or character, as to be preferred in honour before others, and to be greater in the world than they.

For Thy will and the love of Thy glory ought to be

[1] 1 Cor. i. [27, 28].   [2] Ps. xlv. [16].
[3] 1 Thess. ii. [10].   [4] Acts v. [41].

preferred before all things, and to comfort nim more, and please him better, than all the benefits which he either hath received, or may receive.

CHAPTER XXIII

OF FOUR THINGS THAT BRING MUCH INWARD PEACE

My son, now will I teach thee the way of peace and true liberty.

O Lord, I beseech Thee, do as Thou sayest, for this is delightful to me to hear.

BE DESIROUS, MY SON, TO DO THE WILL OF ANOTHER RATHER THAN THINE OWN.[1]

CHOOSE ALWAYS TO HAVE LESS RATHER THAN MORE.[2]

SEEK ALWAYS THE LOWEST PLACE, AND TO BE INFERIOR TO EVERY ONE.[3]

WISH ALWAYS, AND PRAY, THAT THE WILL OF GOD MAY BE WHOLLY FULFILLED IN THEE.[4]

Behold, such a man entereth within the borders of peace and rest.

II. O Lord, this short discourse of Thine containeth within itself much perfection.[5]

It is little to be spoken, but full of meaning, and abundant in fruit.

For if it could faithfully be kept by me, I ought not to be so easily disturbed.

For as often as I feel myself unquiet and weighed down, I find that I have gone back from this doctrine.

But Thou who canst do all things, and ever lovest the profiting of my soul, increase in me Thy grace, that I may be able to fulfil Thy words, and to work out mine own salvation.

[1] Matt. xxvi. [39] ; John v. [30], vi. [38].
[2] 1 Cor. x. [24].   [3] Luke xiv. [10].
[4] Matt. vi. [10].   [5] Matt. v. [48].

A Prayer against evil thoughts.

III. O LORD my God, be not Thou far from me ; my God, have regard to help me : [1] for there have risen up against me sundry thoughts, and great fears, afflicting my soul.

How shall I pass through unhurt ? how shall I break them to pieces ?

' I will go before thee (saith He), and will humble the great ones of the earth ; I will open the doors of the prison, and reveal unto thee hidden secrets.' [2]

Do, O Lord, as Thou sayest, and let all my evil thoughts fly from before Thy face.

This is my hope, my one only consolation, to flee unto Thee in every tribulation, to trust in Thee, to call upon Thee from my inmost heart, and to wait patiently for Thy consolation.

A Prayer for mental illumination.

IV. O merciful JESUS, enlighten Thou me with a clear shining inward light, and remove away all darkness from the habitation of my heart.

Repress Thou my many wandering thoughts, and break in pieces those temptations which violently assault me.

Fight Thou strongly for me, and vanquish the evil beasts, I mean the alluring desires of the flesh ; that so peace may be obtained by Thy power, and that Thine abundant praise may resound in Thy holy court, that is, in a pure conscience.

Command the winds and tempests ; say unto the sea, Be still ; [3] say to the north wind, Blow not ; and there shall be a great calm.

V. Send out Thy light and Thy truth,[4] that they may shine upon the earth ; for until Thou enlighten me, I am but as earth without form and void.

Pour forth Thy grace from above, imbue my heart

---

[1] Psalm lxxi. [12].   [2] Isaiah xlv. [2, 3].
[3] Matt. viii. [26].   [4] Psalm xliii. [3].

with heavenly dew, supply fresh streams of devotion, to
water the face of the earth, that it may bring forth
fruit good and excellent.

Lift Thou up my mind which is pressed down by a
load of sins, and draw up my whole desire to things
heavenly ; that having tasted the sweetness of supernal
happiness, it may be irksome to me even to think
about earthly things.

VI. Do Thou pluck me away, and deliver me from
all transitory consolation of creatures; for no created
thing can give full comfort and rest to my desires.

Join Thou me to Thyself with an inseparable band of
love ; for Thou even alone dost satisfy him that loveth
Thee, and without Thee all things are vain and
frivolous.

CHAPTER XXIV

OF AVOIDING CURIOUS ENQUIRY INTO OTHER MEN'S LIVES

My son, be not curious, nor trouble thyself with idle
anxieties.[1]

What is this or that to thee? follow thou Me.[2]

For what is it to thee, whether that man be such or
such, or whether this man do or speak this or that ?

Thou shalt not need to answer for others, but shalt
give account for thyself;[3] why therefore dost thou
entangle thyself?

Behold, I know every one, and do see all things
that are done under the sun ; also I understand how it
is with every one, what he thinks, what he wishes, and
at what his intentions aim.

Unto Me therefore all things are to be committed ;
but do thou keep thyself gently at peace, and let go
the unquiet, to be as unquiet as they will.

[1] Ecclus. iii. [23] ; 1 Tim. v. [13].   [2] John xxi. [22].
[3] Gal. vi. [4, 5].

Whatsoever they shall have done or said, shall come upon themselves, for Me they cannot deceive.

II. Be not careful for the shadow of a great name, or for the familiar friendship of many, or for the private affection of men.

For these things both distract the heart, and greatly darken it.

Willingly would I speak My word, and reveal My secrets unto thee, if thou wouldest diligently observe My coming, and open unto Me the door of thine heart.

Be thou circumspect, and watchful in prayer, and in all things humble thyself.

CHAPTER XXV

WHEREIN FIRM PEACE OF HEART AND TRUE SPIRITUAL PROGRESS CONSISTETH

My son, I have spoken ; 'Peace I leave with you, My peace I give unto you : not as the world giveth, give I unto you.'[1]

Peace is what all desire, but all do not care for the things that pertain unto true peace.

My peace is with the humble and gentle of heart ; in much patience shall thy peace be.

If thou wilt hear Me and follow My voice, thou shalt be able to enjoy much peace.

What then shall I do, Lord ?

In every matter look to thyself, what thou doest and what thou sayest ; and direct thy whole attention unto this, that thou mayest please Me alone, and neither desire or seek any thing besides Me.

But of the words or deeds of others judge nothing rashly ; neither do thou entangle thyself with things not committed unto thee ; and doing thus thou mayest be little or seldom disturbed.

[1] John xiv. [27].

II. But never to feel any disturbance at all, nor to suffer any trouble of mind or body, belongs not to this life, but to the state of eternal Rest.

Think not therefore that thou hast found true peace, if thou feel no heaviness ; nor that then all is well, if thou art vexed with no adversary ; nor that 'to be perfect,' is to have all things done according to thy desire.

Neither do thou then esteem at all highly of thyself, or account thyself to be specially beloved, if thou be in a state of great devotion and sweetness ; for it is not by these things that a true lover of virtue is known nor doth the [spiritual] progress and perfection of a man consist in these things.

III. WHEREIN then, O Lord, doth it consist ?

IN giving thyself over with all thy heart to the Divine Will, not seeking thine own interest, either in great matters or in small, either in time or in eternity.

So shalt thou keep one and the same countenance, always with thanksgiving, both in prosperity and adversity, weighing all things with an equal balance.

Be thou of such courage, and so patient in hope, that when inward comfort is withdrawn, thou mayest prepare thy heart to suffer even greater things ; and do not justify thyself, as though thou oughtest not to suffer these afflictions or any so great, but justify Me in whatsoever I appoint, and still praise My Holy Name.

Then shalt thou walk in the true and right way of peace, and thou shalt have undoubted hope to see My face again with great delight.

For if thou attain to the full contempt of thyself, know that thou shalt then enjoy abundance of peace, as great as this thy state of sojourning is capable of.

CHAPTER XXVI

OF THE EXCELLENCY OF A FREE MIND, WHICH IS SOONER
GAINED BY HUMBLE PRAYER THAN BY READING

O LORD, it is the business of a perfect man, never to relax his mind from attentive thought of heavenly things, and thus to pass amidst many cares (as it were) without care ; not as one destitute of all feeling, but by the privilege of a free mind, cleaving to no creature with inordinate affection.

II. I beseech Thee, my most gracious God, preserve me from the cares of this life, lest I should be too much entangled therein ; also from the many necessities of the body, lest I should be ensnared by pleasure ; and from whatsoever is an obstacle to the soul, lest being broken with troubles I should be overthrown.

I speak not of those things which worldly vanity so earnestly desireth, but of those miseries, which as punishments and as the common curse of mortality,[1] do weigh down and hinder the soul of Thy servant, that it cannot enter into the freedom of the Spirit, so often as it would.

III. O my God, Thou sweetness ineffable, make bitter for me all carnal comfort, which draws me away from the love of things eternal, and in evil manner allures me to itself by the view of some present delightsome good

Let me not be overcome, O Lord, let me not be overcome by flesh and blood ;[2] let not the world and the brief glory thereof deceive me ; let not the devil and his subtle fraud supplant me.

Give me strength to resist, patience to endure, and constancy to persevere.

Give me instead of all the comforts of the world, the most sweet unction of Thy Spirit, and in place of carnal love, pour in the love of Thy name.

[1] Gen. iii. [17] ; Rom. vii. [23, 24].
[2] Rom. xii. [21].

IV. Behold ! meat, drink, clothes, and other necessaries for the maintenance of the body, are burdensome unto a fervent spirit.

Grant me to use such refreshments moderately, and not to be entangled with an over-great desire of them.

It is not lawful to cast away all things, because nature is to be sustained ; but to require superfluities, and those things that are merely pleasurable, the holy law forbiddeth us ; for then the flesh would rebel against the Spirit. Herein, I beseech Thee, let Thy hand govern me and teach me, that I may not exceed in anything.

CHAPTER XXVII

THAT IT IS PRIVATE LOVE WHICH MOST HINDERETH FROM THE CHIEFEST GOOD

My son, thou oughtest to give all for all, and to be nothing of thyself.

Know thou, that the love of thyself doth thee more hurt than anything in the world.

According to the love and affection which thou bearest towards any thing, so doth it more or less cleave to thee.

If thy love be pure,[1] simple and well-ordered, thou shalt be free from the bondage of things.

Do not covet that which it is not lawful for thee to have. Do not have that which may entangle thee, and deprive thee of inward liberty.

Strange it is that thou committest not thyself wholly unto Me, from the bottom of thy heart, with all things thou canst have or desire.

II. Why dost thou consume thyself with vain grief?[2] why weary thyself with superfluous cares?

Stand to My good will, and thou shalt suffer no detriment at all.

[1] Matt. vi. [22].   [2] Exodus xviii. [18] ; Mic. iv. [9].

If thou seek this or that, and wouldest be in such or such a place, the better to enjoy thy own profit and pleasure, thou shalt never be at quiet, nor free from trouble of mind ; for in every instance somewhat will be wanting, and in every place there will be some one to cross thee.

III. Man's welfare then lies not in obtaining and multiplying any external things, but rather in despising them, and utterly rooting them out from the heart.

And this thou must understand not of income and wealth only, but of seeking after honour also, and the desire of vain praise, all which must pass away with this world.

The place availeth little if the spirit of fervour be wanting, neither shall that peace long continue, which is sought from without ; [1] if the state of thy heart be destitute of a true foundation, that is, unless thou stand steadfast in Me, thou mayest change but not better thyself.

For when occasion arises, and is laid hold of, thou shalt find what thou didst flee from, and more too.

A Prayer for a clean heart, and Heavenly Wisdom.

IV. STRENGTHEN me, O God, by the grace of Thy Holy Spirit.[2]

Grant me to be strengthened with might in the inner man,[3] and to empty my heart of all useless care and anguish ; [4] not to be drawn away with sundry desires of any thing whatever, whether mean or precious, but to look on all things as passing away, and on myself also no less as about to pass away with them.

For nothing is permanent under the sun, where all things are vanity and vexation of spirit.[5] O how wise is he that so considereth them !

V. O Lord, grant me Heavenly wisdom,[6] that I may

---

[1] Isaiah xli. [13].   [2] Psalm li. [12].
[3] Eph. iii. [16].   [4] Matt. vi. [34].
[5] Eccles. i. [14], ii. [17. 26].   [6] Wisd. ix. [4].

learn above all things to seek and to find Thee, above all things to relish and to love Thee, and to think of all other things as being, what indeed they are, at the disposal of Thy wisdom.

Grant me prudently to avoid him that flatters me, and to endure patiently him that contradicts me.

Because it is a great part of wisdom not to be moved with every wind of words,[1] nor to give ear to an ill flattering siren ; for thus we shall go on securely in the way which we have begun.

CHAPTER XXVIII

AGAINST THE TONGUES OF SLANDERERS

My son, take it not grievously if some think ill of thee,[2] and speak that which thou wouldest not willingly hear.

Thou oughtest to judge the worst of thyself, and to think no man weaker than thyself.

If thou dost walk inwardly, thou wilt not much weigh fleeting words outwardly.

It is no small prudence to keep silence in an evil time, and inwardly to turn thyself to Me, and not to be troubled by the judgment of men.

II. Let not thy peace be in the tongues of men ; for whether they interpret well or ill of thee thou art not therefore another man. Where are true peace and true glory ? are they not in Me ?[3]

And he that neither coveteth to please men, nor feareth to displease them, shall enjoy much peace.

From inordinate love and vain fear ariseth all disquietness of heart and distraction of the mind.

[1] Eph. iv. [14].   [2] 1 Cor. iv. [13].
          [3] John xvi. [33].

✗✗ CHAPTER XXIX *U-files Oct- 1915*

HOW WE OUGHT TO CALL UPON GOD, AND TO BLESS HIM, WHEN TRIBULATION IS UPON US

BLESSED be Thy Name, O Lord, for ever ;[1] for that it is Thy will that this temptation and tribulation should come upon me.

I cannot escape it, but must needs flee to Thee, that Thou mayest help me, and turn it to my good.

Lord, I am now in affliction, and my heart is ill at ease, for I am much troubled with the present suffering.

And now, O Beloved Father, what shall I say ?[2] I am caught amidst straits ; save Thou me from this hour.

Yet therefore came I unto this hour, that Thou mayest be glorified, when I shall have been greatly humbled, and by Thee delivered.

Let it please Thee, Lord, to deliver me ;[3] for, poor wretch that I am, what can I do, and whither shall I go without Thee ?

Grant me patience, O Lord, even now in this emergency. Help me, my God, and then I will not fear, how grievously soever I be afflicted.

II. And now amidst these my troubles what shall I say?

Lord, Thy will be done ;[4] I have well deserved to be afflicted and weighed down.

Therefore I ought to bear it ; and O that I may bear it with patience, until the tempest pass over, and all be well again, or even better !

Howbeit Thy Omnipotent hand is able to take even this temptation from me, and to assuage the violence thereof, that I utterly sink not under it ; as oftentimes

---

[1] Job i. [21] ; Psalm cxiii. [2].
[2] Matt xxvi. [or John xii. 27].
[3] Psalm xl. [13].   [4] Matt. vi. [10].

heretofore Thou hast dealt with me, O my God, my Mercy!

And the more difficult it is to me, so much the more easy to Thee is this change of the right hand of the Most High.

/ X   CHAPTER XXX   *U-filer Oct 19 15*

OF CRAVING THE DIVINE AID, AND CONFIDENCE OF RECOVERING GRACE

My son, I am the LORD, that giveth strength in the day of tribulation.[1]

Come thou unto Me, when it is not well with thee.[2]

This is that which most of all hindereth Heavenly consolation, that thou art too slow in turning thyself unto prayer.

For before thou dost earnestly supplicate Me, thou seekest in the meanwhile many comforts, and refreshest thyself in outward things.

And hence it comes to pass that all doth little profit thee, until thou well consider that I am He who do rescue them that trust in Me; and that out of Me, there is neither powerful help, nor profitable counsel, nor lasting remedy.

But do thou, having now recovered breath after the tempest, gather strength again in the light of My mercies; for I am at hand (saith the Lord) to repair all, not only entirely, but also abundantly and in most plentiful measure.

II. Is there any thing hard to Me? or shall I be like one that saith and doeth not?[3]

Where is thy faith? stand firmly and with perseverance; take courage and be patient; comfort will come to thee in due time.

[1] Nahum i. [7].   [2] Matt. xi. [28].
                  [3] Matt. xxiii. [3].

Wait, wait I say, for Me: I will come and take care of thee.

It is a temptation that vexeth thee, and a vain fear that affrighteth thee.

What else doth anxiety about future contingencies bring thee, but sorrow upon sorrow? 'Sufficient for the day is the evil thereof.' [1]

It is a vain thing and unprofitable, to be either disturbed or pleased about future things, which perhaps will never come to pass.

III. But it is incident to man, to be deluded with such imaginations; and a sign of a mind as yet weak, to be so easily drawn away by the suggestions of the Enemy.

For so he may delude and deceive thee, he careth not whether it be by true or by false propositions; nor whether he overthrows thee with the love of present, or the fear of future things.

Let not therefore thy heart be troubled, neither let it fear.

Trust in Me, and put thy confidence in My mercy. [2]

When thou thinkest thyself farthest off from Me, oftentimes I am nearest unto thee.

When thou countest almost all to be lost, then oftentimes the greatest gain of reward is close at hand.

All is not lost, when any thing falleth out contrary.

Thou oughtest not to judge according to present feeling; nor so to take any grief, or give thyself over to it, from whencesoever it cometh, as though all hopes of escape were quite taken away.

IV. Think not thyself wholly left, although for a time I have sent thee some tribulation, or even have withdrawn thy desired comfort; for this is the way to the Kingdom of Heaven.

And without doubt it is more expedient for thee and the rest of My servants, that ye be exercised with adversities, than that ye should have all things according to your desires.

---

[1] Matt. vi. [34].   [2] Psalm xci. [2].

I know the secret thoughts of thy heart, and that it is very expedient for thy welfare, that thou be left sometimes without taste [of spiritual sweetness, and in a dry condition], lest perhaps thou shouldest be puffed up with thy prosperous estate, and shouldest be willing to please thyself in that which thou art not.

That which I have given, I can take away; and I can restore it again when I please.

V. When I give it, it is Mine; when I withdraw it, I take not any thing that is thine; for Mine is every good gift and every perfect gift.[1]

If I send upon thee affliction, or any cross whatever, repine not, nor let thy heart fail thee; I can quickly succour thee, and turn all thy heaviness into joy.

Howbeit I am righteous, and greatly to be praised when I deal thus with thee.

VI. If thou art wise, and considerest what the truth is, thou never oughtest to mourn dejectedly for any adversity that befalleth thee, but rather to rejoice and give thanks.

Yea, thou wilt account this time especial joy, that I afflict thee with sorrows, and do not spare thee.

'As the Father hath loved Me, I also love you,'[2] said I unto My beloved disciples; whom certainly I sent not out to temporal joys, but to great conflicts; not to honours, but to contempts; not to idleness, but to labours; not to rest, but to bring forth much fruit with patience. Remember thou these words, O my son!

CHAPTER XXXI

OF THE CONTEMPT OF ALL CREATURES, TO FIND OUT THE CREATOR

O Lord, I stand much in need of yet greater grace, if I ought to reach that pitch, where neither man nor any creature shall be a hindrance unto me.

---

[1] James i. [17].   [2] John xv. [9].

For as long as any thing holds me back, I cannot freely take my flight to Thee.

He was longing to fly freely who said, 'O that I had wings like a dove, and I will flee away and be at rest !' [1]

What is more at rest than the single eye ? [2] and what is more free than he that desireth nothing upon earth ?

A man ought therefore to mount over all creatures, and perfectly to go out of himself and stand in a sort of ecstacy of mind, and to see that Thou, the Creator of all things, hast nothing amongst creatures like unto Thyself.

Unless too a man be set free from all creatures, he cannot with freedom of mind attend unto divine things.

For that is the reason why there are few contemplative men to be found, because few have the knowledge to withdraw themselves fully from perishing creatures.

II. To obtain this there is need of much grace, which may elevate the soul, and carry it away above itself.

And unless a man be elevated in spirit, and freed from all creatures, and wholly united unto God, whatsoever he knoweth, and whatsoever he hath, is of no great weight.

For a long while shall he be small, and lie grovelling below, whoever he be that esteemeth any thing great, but the One only Infinite Eternal Good.

And whatsoever is not God, is nothing, and ought to be accounted as nothing.

There is great difference between the wisdom of an illuminated and devout man, and the knowledge of a learned and studious clerk.

Far more noble is that learning which floweth from above, from the Divine influence, than that which is painfully acquired by the wit of man.

III. There are many that desire contemplation, but they have no mind to practise the things that are required thereunto.

[1] Psalm. lv. [6].   [2] Matt. vi. [22].

K

It is also a great hindrance, that men rest in signs and sensible things, and take little care about the perfect mortification of themselves.

I know not what it is, or by what spirit we are led, or what we pretend, we that seem to be called spiritual, that we take so much pains, and are so full of anxiety about transitory and mean things, while we scarcely at all, or but seldom, think of our own inward concernments, with full recollection of mind.

IV. Alas, presently after a slight recollection we break out again, and weigh not our works with diligent and strict examination.

We mind not where our affections lie, nor bewail the impurity that is in all our actions.

For 'all flesh had corrupted his way,' and therefore did the great deluge ensue.[1]

Since then our inward affection is much corrupted, our actions thence proceeding must needs be corrupted also, giving proof of the want of internal vigour.

From a pure heart proceedeth the fruit of a good life.

V. We ask how much a man has done, but from what degree of virtuous principle he acts, is not so carefully weighed.

We enquire whether he has been courageous, rich, handsome, skilful, a good writer, a good singer, or a good labourer; but how poor he is in spirit, how patient and meek, how devout and spiritual, is seldom spoken of.

Nature respecteth the outward things of a man. Grace turneth itself to the inward.

The one is often disappointed; the other hath her trust in God, and so is not deceived.

[1] Gen. vi. [12], vii. [21].

CHAPTER XXXII

OF SELF-DENIAL, AND RENOUNCING EVERY EVIL APPETITE

My son, thou canst not possess perfect liberty unless thou wholly renounce thyself.[1]

They are but in fetters, all who merely seek their own interest, and are lovers of themselves; covetous are they, inquisitive, gossiping, always seeking what is soft and delicate, not the things of Jesus Christ, but oftentimes devising and framing that which will not continue.

For all that is not of God shall perish.

Keep this short and complete saying: 'Forsake all and thou shalt find all.' Leave concupiscence and thou shalt find rest.

Weigh this thoroughly in thy mind, and when thou hast fulfilled it, thou shalt understand all things.

II. O Lord, this is not the work of one day, nor children's sport; yea rather in this short word is included all the perfection of religious persons.

III. My son, thou oughtest not to turn away, nor at once to be cast down, when thou hearest of the way of the perfect; but shouldest rather be stirred up to higher things, at least in desire to sigh after them.

I would it were so with thee, and thou wert arrived at this, to be no longer a lover of thyself, but didst stand merely at My beck, and at his whom I have appointed a father over thee; then shouldest thou exceedingly please Me, and all thy life would pass away in joy and peace.

Thou hast yet many things to part with, which unless thou wholly resign up unto Me, thou shalt not attain to that which thou desirest.

'I counsel thee to buy of Me gold tried in the fire,

[1] Matt. xvi. [24], xix. [21].

that thou mayest become rich ; " [1] that is, Heavenly Wisdom, which treadeth under foot all that is mean and low.

Set little by earthly wisdom, and care not fondly to please others or thyself.

IV. I said, that mean things must be bought with things which, among men, are precious and of great esteem.

For true Heavenly Wisdom doth seem very mean, of small account, and almost forgotten among men, as having no high thoughts of itself, nor seeking to be magnified upon earth. Many indeed praise it with their mouth, but in their life they are far from it ; yet is it the precious pearl,[2] which is hidden from many.

CHAPTER XXXIII

OF INCONSTANCY OF HEART, AND OF HAVING OUR FINAL INTENTIONS DIRECTED UNTO GOD

My son, trust not to thy feeling, for whatever it be now, it will quickly be changed into another thing.

As long as thou livest, thou art subject to mutability,[3] even against thy will ; so as thou art found one while merry, another while sad ; one while quiet, another while troubled ; now devout, then indevout ; now diligent, then listless ; now grave, and then light.

But he that is wise and well instructed in the Spirit standeth fast upon these mutable things ; not heeding what he feeleth in himself, or which way the wind of instability bloweth ; but so that the whole intention of his mind tendeth to the right and best end.

For thus he will be able to continue throughout one and the self-same, and unshaken ; in the midst of so

----

[1] Rev. iii. [18].   [2] Matt. xiii. [46].

[3] Job xiv. [2].

many various events the single eye of his intention being directed unceasingly towards Me.

II. And the purer the eye of the intention is,[1] with so much the more constancy doth a man pass through the several kinds of storms which assail him.

But in many the eye of a pure intention waxes dim, for their regard is quickly drawn aside to some pleasurable object which meets them.

For it is rare to find one who is wholly free from all blemish of self-seeking.

So of old the Jews came to Bethany to Martha and Mary, not for JESUS' sake only, but that they might see Lazarus also.[2]

The eye of our intention therefore is to be purified, that it may be single and right,[3] and is to be directed towards Me, beyond all the various objects which may come between.

CHAPTER XXXIV

THAT GOD IS SWEET ABOVE ALL THINGS, AND IN ALL THINGS, TO HIM THAT LOVETH HIM

'BEHOLD! My God, and all things [to me].' What can I wish more, and what happier thing can I long for?

O sweet and savoury word! to him, that is, who loveth the word, not the world nor the things that are in the world.

'My God, and all things.' To him that understandeth, enough is said; and to repeat it often, is delightful to him that loveth.

Forasmuch as when Thou art present, all things are delightful, but when Thou art absent, every thing becomes irksome.

[1] Matt. vi. [22].   [2] John xii. [9].
[3] Matt. vi. [22].

Thou givest quietness of heart, and great peace, and festive joy.

Thou makest us to think well of all circumstances, and in all to praise Thee ; neither can any thing please long without Thee ; but if it must needs be pleasant and tasteful, Thy Grace must be present, and it must be seasoned with the seasoning of Thy Wisdom.

II. What will not be tasteful unto him that hath a true relish for Thee ?

And him that hath no relish for Thee, what shall have power to please ?

But the wise men of the world, and they also who relish the things of the flesh, are destitute of Thy wisdom ;[1] for in the former is found the utmost vanity, and in the latter death.

But they that follow Thee by the contempt of worldly things, and mortification of the flesh, are known to be truly wise ; for they are brought over from vanity to truth, from the flesh to the spirit.

These relish God ; and what good soever is found in creatures, they wholly refer unto the praise of their Maker.

Great, however, yea, very great is the difference between the sweetness of the Creator and of the creature, of Eternity and of time, of Light uncreated and of light enlightened.

III. O Everlasting Light, surpassing all created luminaries, dart Thou the beams of Thy brightness from above, which may penetrate all the most inward parts of my heart.

Purify, rejoice, enlighten and enliven my spirit, with all the powers thereof, that I may cleave unto Thee with most exceeding joy and triumph.

O when will that blessed and desired hour come, that Thou mayest satisfy me with Thy Presence, and be unto me All in all.

So long as this is not granted me, I shall not have full joy.

---

[1] 1 Cor. i. [26] ; Rom. viii. [5] ; 1 John ii. [16].

Still, alas! the old Man doth live in me,[1] he is not wholly crucified, is not perfectly dead.

Still lusteth he mightily against the Spirit, and stirreth up inward wars, nor suffereth the kingdom of the soul to be in peace.

IV. But Thou that rulest the power of the sea, and stillest the violent motion of its waves,[2] arise and help me!

Scatter the nations that desire war;[3] crush Thou them in Thy might.

Display Thy wonderful works, I beseech Thee, and let Thy right hand be glorified: for there is no other hope or refuge for me, save in Thee, O Lord my God.[4]

CHAPTER XXXV

THAT THERE IS NO SECURITY FROM TEMPTATION IN THIS LIFE

My son, thou art never secure in this life, but, as long as thou livest,[5] thou shalt always need spiritual armour.

Thou dwellest among enemies, and art assaulted on the right hand and on the left.[6]

If therefore thou defend not thyself on every side with the shield of patience, thou wilt not be long without a wound.

Moreover, if thou set not thy heart fixedly on Me, with a sincere wish to suffer all things for Me, thou wilt not be able to bear the heat of this combat, nor to attain to the palm of the blessed.

Thou oughtest therefore manfully to go through all, and to use a strong hand against whatsoever withstandeth thee.

[1] Rom. vii.   [2] Psalm lxxxix. [9].   [3] Psalm lxviii. [30].
[4] Psalm xxxi. [14].   [5] Job vii. [1].   [6] 2 Cor. vi. [7].

For to him that overcometh is Manna given, and for the indolent there remaineth much misery.

II. If thou seek rest in this life, how wilt thou then attain to the everlasting Rest?

Dispose not thyself for much rest, but for great patience.

Seek true peace, not in earth, but in Heaven ; not in men, nor in any other creature, but in God alone.

For the love of God thou oughtest cheerfully to undergo all things, that is to say, all labour and pain, temptation, vexation, anxiety, necessity, infirmity, injury, obloquy, reproof, humiliation, confusion, correction, and scorn.

These help to virtue ; these are the trial of a novice in Christ ; these frame the Heavenly Crown.

I will give an everlasting reward for a short labour, and infinite glory for transitory confusion.

III. Thinkest thou that thou shalt always have spiritual consolations at thine own will?

My saints had not such always, but they had many afflictions, and sundry temptations, and feelings of great desolateness.

Nevertheless in all these they bore themselves up patiently, and trusted rather in God than in themselves ; knowing that the sufferings of this time are not worthy to be compared with the future glory.[1]

Wilt thou have that at once, which many after many tears and great labours have hardly obtained?

Wait for the Lord, behave thyself manfully, and be of good courage ;[2] do not distrust [Him], do not leave thy place, but steadily expose both body and soul for the glory of God.

I will reward thee in most plentiful manner ; I will be with thee in every tribulation.

---

[1] Rom. viii. [18].   [2] Psalm xxvii. [14].

CHAPTER XXXVI

AGAINST THE VAIN JUDGMENTS OF MEN

My son, cast thy heart firmly on the Lord, and fear not the judgment of men, when conscience testifieth of thy dutifulness and innocency.

It is a good and happy thing to suffer in such a way; nor will this be grievous to a heart which is humble, and which trusteth rather in God than in itself.

The most part of men are given to talk much, and therefore little confidence is to be placed in them.

Moreover also, to satisfy all is not possible.

Although Paul endeavoured to please all in the Lord, and was made all things to all men,[1] yet with him it was a very small thing that he should be judged of man's judgment.[2]

II. He did abundantly for the edification and salvation of others as much as lay in his power to do;[3] yet could he not hinder but that he was by others sometimes judged, sometimes despised.

Therefore he committed all to God, who knew all; and when men spake unjust things, or thought vanities and lies, and boasted themselves as they listed, he defended himself, even to their face, with humility and patience.

Sometimes however he made answer, lest the weak should be offended by his silence.[4]

III. Who art thou that thou shouldest fear a mortal man? to-day he is, and to-morrow he is not seen.[5]

Fear God, and thou shalt not shrink from the terrors of men.

What harm can the words or injuries of any man do thee? he hurteth himself rather than thee, nor shall

---

[1] 1 Cor. ix. [22].   [2] 1 Cor. iv. [3].   [3] Col. i. [29].
[4] Acts xxvi.; Phil. i. [14].   [5] 1 Mac. ii. [62, 63].

he be able to avoid the judgment of God[1] whosoever he be.

Do thou have God before thine eyes, and contend not with peevish words.

And though for the present thou seem to be worsted, and to suffer shame undeservedly, do not therefore repine, neither do thou lessen thy crown by impatience.[2]

But rather lift thou up thine eyes unto Me in Heaven, who am able to deliver thee from all shame and wrong, and to render to every man according to his works.

CHAPTER XXXVII

OF PURE AND ENTIRE RESIGNATION OF OURSELVES, FOR THE OBTAINING FREEDOM OF HEART

My son, forsake thyself, and thou shalt find Me.[3]

Stay where thou art, making no choice, nor appropriating any thing whatever to thyself; and thou shalt always be a gainer.

For even greater grace shall be added to thee, the moment thou dost resign thyself, provided thou dost not turn back to take thyself again.

Lord, how often shall I resign myself? and wherein shall I forsake myself?

Always, yea, every hour; as well in small things as in great. I except nothing, but do desire that thou be found stripped of all things.

Otherwise, how canst thou be Mine, and I thine, unless thou be stript of all self-will, both within and without?

---

[1] Rom. ii. [3] ; 1 Cor. xi. [32].   [2] Heb. xii. [1, 2].
[3] Matt. xvi. [24].

The sooner thou doest this, the better it will be with thee ; and the more fully and sincerely thou doest it, so much the more shalt thou please Me, and so much the greater shall be thy gain.

II. Some there are who resign themselves, but with certain exceptions : for they put not their full trust in God, and therefore they study how to provide for themselves.

Some also at first do offer all, but afterwards being assailed with temptation, they return again to their own ways, and therefore make no progress in the path of virtue.

These shall not attain to the true liberty of a pure heart, nor to the favour of My sweetest familiarity, unless they first make an entire resignation and a daily oblation of themselves. Without this, there neither is nor can be any lasting fruitful union.

III. I have very often said unto thee, and now again I say the same, Forsake thyself,[1] resign thyself, and thou shalt enjoy much inward peace.

Give all for all ; ask for nothing, require back nothing ; abide purely and unhesitatingly in Me, and thou shalt possess Me ; thou shalt be free in heart, and darkness shall not tread thee down.

Let this be thy whole endeavour, this thy prayer, this thy desire ; that thou mayest be stript of all selfishness, and with entire simplicity follow Jesus only ; mayest die to thyself, and live eternally to Me.

Then shalt thou be rid of all vain fancies, causeless perturbations, and superfluous cares.

Then also immoderate fear shall leave thee, and inordinate love shall die.

[1] Matt. xvi. [24].

CHAPTER XXXVIII

OF GOOD GOVERNMENT IN THINGS EXTERNAL, AND OF HAVING RECOURSE TO GOD IN DANGERS

My son, thou oughtest with all diligence to endeavour, that in every place, and in every external action or occupation, thou mayest be inwardly free, and thoroughly master of thyself; and that all things be under thee, and not thou under them.

Thou must be lord and master of thine own actions, and not be a slave or a hireling.

Rather thou shouldest be as a freed man and a true Hebrew, passing over into the lot and freedom of the sons of God.

For they standing upon things present, contemplate things eternal.

With the left eye they look on transitory things, and with the right on the things of heaven.

They are not drawn by temporal things to cleave unto them; rather they draw temporal things to serve them well, in such ways as they are ordained by God, and appointed by the Great Work-master, who hath left nothing in His creation without due order.

II. If too in all circumstances thou stand stedfast, and do not estimate the things which thou seest and hearest by the outward appearance, nor with a carnal eye; but presently in every affair dost enter with Moses into the Tabernacle[1] to ask counsel of the Lord; thou shalt sometimes hear the Divine Oracle, and shalt return instructed concerning many things, both present and to come.

For Moses always had recourse to the Tabernacle for the deciding of doubts and questions, and fled to the help of prayer, for support under dangers and the iniquity of men.

[1] Exod. xxxiii. [9].

So oughtest thou in like manner to take refuge within the closet of thine heart,[1] very earnestly craving the Divine favour.

For we read, that for this cause Joshua and the children of Israel were deceived by the Gibeonites, because they asked not counsel beforehand at the mouth of the Lord,[2] but trusting too easily to fair words, were deluded by counterfeit pity.

CHAPTER XXXIX

THAT A MAN SHOULD NOT BE FRETFUL IN MATTERS OF BUSINESS

My son, always commit thy cause to Me, I will dispose well of it in due time.

Wait for My ordering of it, and thou shalt find it will be for thy good.

O LORD, I do most cheerfully commit all unto Thee, for my care can little avail.

Would that I did not so much dwell on future events, but gave myself up without reluctance to Thy good pleasure.

II. My son, oftentimes a man vehemently struggleth for somewhat he desireth, but when he hath arrived at it, he beginneth to be of another mind; for the affections do not long remain on one object, but rather urge us from one thing to another.

It is therefore no small benefit for a man to forsake himself even in the smallest things.

III. The true profiting of a man consisteth in the denying of himself; and he that is thus self-denied, liveth in great freedom and security.

But the old Enemy,[3] who always sets himself against

---

[1] Matt. vi. [6].   [2] Josh. ix. [14].   [3] 1 Pet. v. [8].

all that are good, ceaseth at no time from tempting, but day and night lieth grievously in wait, to cast the unwary, if he can, headlong into the snare of deceit.

'Watch ye, and pray,' saith the Lord, 'that ye enter not into temptation.'[1]

CHAPTER XL

THAT MAN HATH NO GOOD OF HIMSELF, NOR ANY THING WHEREOF HE CAN GLORY

'Lord, what is man, that Thou art mindful of him, or the son of man, that Thou visitest him?'[2]

What hath man deserved, that Thou shouldest grant him Thy favour?

O Lord, what cause can I have to complain, if Thou forsake me? or if Thou do not that which I desire, what can I justly say against it?

Surely this I may truly think and say; Lord, I am nothing, I can do nothing, I have nothing that is good of myself, but in all things I am full of decay, and am ever tending to nothing.

And unless Thou help me, and inwardly inform me, I become altogether lukewarm and ready to fall to pieces.

II. But Thou, Lord, art Thyself always The Same, and endurest for ever;[3] always Good, Just, and Holy; doing all things well, justly, and holily, and ordering them in wisdom.

Whereas I that am more ready to go backward than forward, do not ever continue in one estate, for 'seven times are passed over me.'[4]

Nevertheless it soon becometh better, when it so pleaseth Thee, and when Thou vouchsafest to stretch forth Thy helping hand; for Thou canst help me alone

---

[1] Matt. xxvi. [41].   [2] Psalm viii. [4].
[3] Psalm cii. [12].   [4] Dan. iv. [16, 23, 32].

without human aid, and so strengthen me, that my countenance shall be no more changed, but my heart shall be turned to Thee alone, and be at rest.

III. Wherefore, if I could once perfectly cast off all human consolation, either for the attainment of devotion, or because of mine own necessities, which enforce me to seek after Thee, (for no mortal man can comfort me,) then might I well hope in Thy grace, and rejoice in the gift of new consolation.

IV. Thanks be unto Thee, from whom all proceedeth, whensoever it goes well with me.

But I am in Thy sight mere vanity and nothing, an unconstant and weak person.

Whereof then can I glory; or for what do I desire to be respected? is it for being nothing? this too is most vain.

Mere empty glory is in truth an evil pest, the greatest of vanities; because it draweth a man from true glory, and robbeth him of Heavenly Grace.

For whilst he pleaseth himself, he displeaseth Thee; whilst he gapeth after the praise of men, he is deprived of true virtues.

V. But the true glory and holy exultation is for a man to glory in Thee,[1] and not in himself; to rejoice in Thy name, not in his own virtue, nor to take delight in any creature except it be for Thy sake.

Praised be Thy Name, not mine; magnified be Thy work, not mine: let Thy Holy Name be blessed, but to me let no part of men's praises be given.[2]

Thou art my glory, Thou art the joy of my heart.

In Thee will I glory and rejoice all the day, but as for myself, I will not glory, but in mine infirmities.

VI. Let the Jews seek honour one of another,[3] I will ask for that which cometh from God alone.

Truly all human glory, all temporal honour, all worldly highness, compared to Thy eternal glory, is vanity and folly.

---

[1] Hab. iii. [18].   [2] Ps. cxiii. [3]; cxv. [1].
[3] John v. [44].

O my God, my Truth, and my Mercy, O Blessed Trinity, to Thee alone be praise, honour, power and glory, for ever and ever.

CHAPTER XLI

OF THE CONTEMPT OF ALL TEMPORAL HONOUR

My son, make it no matter of thine, if thou see others honoured and advanced, but thyself contemned and debased.

Lift up thy heart into Heaven to Me, and the contempt of men on earth will not grieve thee.

Lord, we are in blindness, and are quickly misled by vanity.

If I look rightly into myself, I cannot say that any creature hath ever done me wrong ; and therefore I cannot justly complain before Thee.

II. But because I have often and grievously sinned against Thee, all creatures do justly take arms against me.

Unto me, therefore, shame and contempt are justly due, but unto Thee praise, honour, and glory.

And unless I prepare myself with cheerful willingness to be despised and forsaken of all creatures, and to be esteemed quite entirely nothing, I cannot obtain inward peace and stability, nor be spiritually enlightened, nor be fully united unto Thee.

CHAPTER XLII

THAT OUR PEACE IS NOT TO BE SET ON MEN

My son, if thou rest thy peace on any person, because thou hast formed a high opinion of him, and because you are in daily familiar intercourse with each other, thou wilt become entangled and unstable.

But if thou have recourse unto the ever-living and abiding Truth, the desertion or death of a friend will not grieve thee.

Thy regard for thy friend ought to be grounded in Me; and for My sake is he to be beloved, whosoever he be that thou thinkest well of, and who is very dear unto thee in this life.

Without Me friendship hath no strength, no continuance; neither is that love true and pure, which is not knit by Me.

Thou oughtest to be so dead to such affections of beloved friends, that (so far as thou art concerned) thou wouldest choose to be without all human sympathy.

Man approacheth so much the nearer unto God, the farther he retireth from all earthly comfort.

In proportion, too, as he descendeth lower into himself, and is meaner in his own sight, so much the higher he ascendeth unto God.

II. But he that attributeth any good unto himself, hindereth God's grace from coming unto him; because the Grace of the HOLY SPIRIT ever seeketh an humble heart.[1]

If thou couldest but perfectly annihilate thyself, and empty thyself of all created love, then might I even hold Myself bound to overflow into thee with great Grace.

When thou lookest to the creatures, the countenance of the Creator is withdrawn from thee.

[1] 1 Pet. v. [5].

L

Learn in all things to overcome thyself, for the sake of thy Creator; then shalt thou be able to attain unto divine knowledge.

How mean soever any thing be, if it is inordinately loved and regarded, it keeps back [the soul] from the Chiefest Good, and corrupts it.

CHAPTER XLIII

AGAINST VAIN AND SECULAR KNOWLEDGE

My son, let not the sayings of men move thee, however fair and ingenious they may be. 'For the Kingdom of God consisteth not in word, but in power.'[1]

Give attention to My words, for they inflame the heart, and enlighten the mind; they produce compunction, and they supply abundant variety of consolation.

Never read thou the word of God in order to appear more learned or more wise.

Be studious for the mortification of thy sins; for this will profit thee more than the knowledge of many difficult questions.

II. When thou shalt have read and known many things, thou must needs ever return to one Beginning and Principle.

I am He that teacheth man knowledge; and I bestow on little children a clearer understanding than can be taught by man.

He to whom I speak, shall quickly be wise, and shall profit much in the Spirit.

Woe be to them that enquire many curious things of men, and take small care about the way of serving Me!

The time will come, when the Master of masters,

[1] 1 Cor. iv. [20].

Christ the Lord of Angels, shall appear, to hear the lessons of all, that is, to examine the consciences of every one.

And then will He search Jerusalem with candles, and the hidden things of darkness shall be laid open,[1] and the arguings of men's tongues shall be silent.

III. I am He who in one instant do lift up the humble mind, to comprehend more reasonings of eternal Truth, than if one had studied ten years in the schools.

I teach without noise of words, without confusion of opinions, without ambition of honour, without the scuffling of arguments.

I am He who instruct men to despise earthly things, to loath things present, to seek things eternal, to relish things eternal ; to flee honours, to endure offences, to place all hope in Me, out of Me to desire nothing, and above all things ardently to love Me.

IV. For a certain person, by loving Me from the bottom of his heart, became instructed in things divine, and was wont to speak admirable truths.

He made greater progress by forsaking all things, than by studying subtle niceties.

Nevertheless, to some men I speak common things, to others things special ; to some I gently shew Myself in signs and figures, whilst to some I reveal mysteries in much light.

The voice of books is indeed one, but it informs not all alike ; for inwardly I am the teacher of the Truth, the searcher of the heart, the discerner of the thoughts, the promoter of the actions, distributing to every man as I shall judge meet.

[1] Zeph. i. [12] ; 1 Cor. iv. [5].

CHAPTER XLIV

OF NOT FETCHING TROUBLE TO OURSELVES FROM OUTWARD THINGS

My son, in many things it is thy duty to be ignorant, and to esteem thyself as one dead upon the earth, and to whom the whole world is crucified.[1]

Many things too there are which it is thy duty to pass by with a deaf ear, that so thou mayest be more mindful of those which belong unto thy peace.

It is more profitable to turn away one's eyes from unpleasing subjects, and to leave each person to his own opinion, than to give attendance to contentious discourses.

If all stand well betwixt God and thee, and thou hast His judgment in thy mind, thou shalt very easily endure to be as one defeated.

II. O Lord, to what a pass are we come! Behold, we bewail a temporal loss, for a pitiful gain we toil and run; while the spiritual harm we incur is forgotten, and hardly at last do we return to a sense of it.

That which little or nothing profiteth, is minded, and that which is especially necessary, is negligently passed over; because the whole man doth slide off to external things, and unless he speedily recover himself, he settleth down in them, and that willingly.

[1] Gal. vi. [14].

CHAPTER XLV

THAT CREDIT IS NOT TO BE GIVEN TO ALL, AND THAT MAN IS PRONE TO OFFEND IN WORDS

GRANT me help, O Lord, in tribulation, for vain is the help of man ![1]

How often have I not met with faithfulness there, where I thought myself sure of it !

How often too have I found it there, where beforehand I least expected it !

It is vain therefore to have hope in men ; but the salvation of the righteous is in Thee, O God !

Blessed be Thou, O Lord my God, in all things that befall us.

We are weak and unstable ; quickly are we deceived and quite changed.

II. Who is he, that is able in all things so warily and circumspectly to keep himself, as never to come into any deception or perplexity ?

But he that trusteth in Thee, O Lord, and seeketh Thee with a single heart, doth not so easily slip.[2]

And if he fall into any tribulation, be he never so much entangled, yet shall he quickly either through Thee be delivered, or by Thee be comforted ; for Thou wilt not forsake him that hopeth in Thee even to the end.

A friend is rare to be found, that continueth faithful in all his friend's distresses.

Thou, O Lord, even Thou alone art most faithful at all times, and there is none other like unto Thee.

III. O how wise was that holy soul which said, ' My mind is firmly settled, and is grounded in Christ.'

If thus it were with me, the fear of man would not so easily vex me, nor darts of words move me.

Who has the power to foresee, who to guard against,

---

[1] Psalm lx. [11]. [2] Prov. x. [29].

all future evils? If even when we do foresee things, they oftentimes hurt us, how can unforeseen evils otherwise than grievously wound us?

But wretch as I am, why have I not foreseen better for myself? why too have I so easily given credit to others?

But we are men, nothing else but frail men, even though by many we were to be reputed and called Angels.

Whom shall I trust, O Lord? whom shall I trust but Thee? Thou art the Truth, which neither doth deceive, nor can be deceived.

And on the other side, 'every man is a liar,'[1] weak, unconstant, and subject to fall, especially in words; and therefore we must scarce ever immediately give credit to that which on the face of it seemeth to sound right.

IV. O with what wisdom hast thou warned us to beware of men; and, that a man's foes are they of his own household;[2] and not to give credit, if one should say, Lo here, or Lo there.

My hurt has been my instructor, and I wish it may make me more cautious, and not more unwise.

'Be wary,' saith one, 'be wary, keep to thyself what I say to thee;' and whilst I hold my peace, and think it is secret, he cannot himself keep that which he desired me to keep, but presently betrays both me and himself, and is gone.

From such mischief-making, reckless persons protect Thou me, O Lord, that I neither fall into their hands, nor ever commit such things myself.

Grant me to observe truth and constancy in my words, and to remove far from me a crafty tongue.

What I am not willing to suffer I ought by all means to beware of doing.

V. O how good is it and tending to peace, to be silent about other men, and not to believe indifferently all that is said, nor too easily to hand on reports.[3]

---

[1] Rom. iii. [4].   [2] Mic. vii. [6].   [3] Prov. xxv. [9].

[How good it is] to lay one's self open to few ; and ever to be seeking after Thee as the beholder of the heart :[1]

And not to be carried about with every wind of words, but to desire that all things both within and without, be accomplished according to the pleasure of Thy will.

How safe is it, for the keeping of heavenly Grace, to avoid appearances, and not to seek those things which seem to cause admiration abroad ; but to pursue with all diligence the things which bring amendment of life and godly zeal.

VI. How many have been the worse for having their virtue known and over-hastily commended !

How truly profitable hath grace been when preserved in silence, in this frail life, which we are told is all temptation, and warfare !

CHAPTER XLVI

OF PUTTING OUR TRUST IN GOD WHEN EVIL WORDS ARISE

My son, stand steadily, and put thy trust in Me ;[2] for what are words, but words ?

They fly through the air, but a stone they cannot hurt.

If thou art guilty, think that thou wouldest gladly amend thyself; if conscience reproach thee not, consider that thou wouldest gladly suffer this for God's sake.

Little enough it is, to suffer sometimes from words, since thou hast not yet the courage to endure hard stripes.

And why do such small matters go to thy heart, but because thou art yet carnal, and regardest men more than thou oughtest?

[1] Isaiah xxvi. [3].　　　　[2] Psalm xxxvii. [3].

For it is because thou art afraid of being despised, that thou art unwilling to be reproved for thy faults, and seekest the shelter of excuses.

II. But look better into thyself, and thou shalt acknowledge that the world is yet alive in thee, and a vain desire to please men.

For when thou shrinkest from being abased and confounded for thy faults, it is evident thou art neither truly humble, nor truly dead to the world, nor the world crucified to thee.

But do thou give diligent ear to My word, and thou shalt not care for ten thousand words spoken by men.

Behold, if all should be spoken against thee that could be most maliciously invented, what would it hurt thee, if thou wouldst suffer it to pass entirely away, and make no more reckoning of it than of a mote? could it pluck so much as one hair from thy head? [1]

III. But he that hath no heart within him, nor hath God before his eyes, is easily moved with a word of dispraise.

Whereas he that trusteth in Me, and hath no wish to confide in his own judgment, shall be free from the fear of men.

For I am the Judge [2] and the discerner of all secrets : I well understand how the matter passed ; I know him that offereth the injury, and him that suffereth it.

From Me proceedeth that word ; by My permission this hath happened ; that the thoughts of many hearts may be revealed. [3]

I shall judge the guilty, and the innocent ; but by a secret judgment I have thought fit beforehand to prove them both.

IV. The testimony of men oftentimes deceiveth : My judgment is true ; it shall stand, and shall not be overthrown :

It commonly lieth hid, and is manifest but to few, and that in special cases : yet it never erreth, nor can

---

[1] Matt. x. [30] ; Luke xii. [7].
[2] Psalm vii. [8].   [3] Luke ii. [35].

err, although to the eyes of the foolish it may seem not right.

To Me therefore men ought to have recourse in every judgment, and not to lean on their own opinion.

For the just man will not be disturbed,[1] whatsoever befalleth him from God.   Even if an unjust charge be brought against him, he will not much care.

Nor again will he vainly exult, if through others he be justly vindicated.

For he considereth that I am He that searcheth the hearts and reins,[2] and do judge not according to the outward face, and human appearance.

For oftentimes that in My sight is found worthy of blame, which in the judgment of men is thought to be commendable.

V. O Lord God, the just judge, strong and patient, Thou who knowest the frailty and wickedness of men, be Thou my strength, and all my confidence, for mine own conscience sufficeth me not.

Thou knowest what I know not; and therefore under all blame I ought to humble myself, and to bear it meekly.

Of Thy mercy then forgive me whenever I have acted otherwise, and when the next trial comes, grant me the grace of more thorough endurance.   Because better to me is Thine overflowing pity for the obtaining of pardon, than any fancied righteousness of my own to ward off the latent misgivings of conscience.

Although I know nothing by myself,[3] yet I cannot hereby justify myself; for without Thy mercy, in Thy sight shall no man living be justified.[4]

[1] Prov. xii. [13].   [2] Psalm vii. [9]; Rev. ii. [23].
[3] 1 Cor. iv. [4].   [4] Psalm cxliii. [2].

CHAPTER XLVII

THAT ALL GRIEVOUS THINGS ARE TO BE ENDURED FOR THE SAKE OF ETERNAL LIFE

My son, be not wearied out by the labours which thou hast undertaken for My sake, nor let tribulations cast thee down ever at all; but let My promise strengthen and comfort thee under every circumstance.

I am well able to reward thee, above all measure and degree.

Thou shalt not long toil here, nor always be oppressed with griefs.

Wait a little while, and thou shalt see a speedy end of thine evils.

There will come an hour when all labour and trouble shall cease.

Poor and brief is all that which passeth away with time.

II. Do in earnest what thou doest; labour faithfully in My vineyard; [1] I will be thy recompence.

Write, read, chant, mourn, keep silence, pray, endure crosses manfully; life everlasting is worth all these conflicts, and greater than these.

Peace shall come in one day which is known unto the Lord, and it shall be not day nor night, [2] (that is, of this present time,) but unceasing light, infinite brightness, stedfast peace, and secure rest.

Then thou shalt not say, 'Who shall deliver me from the body of this death?' [3] nor cry, 'Woe is me, that my sojourning is prolonged!' [4] for death shall be cast down headlong, and there shall be salvation which can never fail, no more anxiety, blessed joy, society sweet and noble.

III. O if thou hadst seen the everlasting crowns of the Saints in heaven, [5] and with how great glory they

---

[1] Matt. xx. [7].   [2] Zech. xiv. [7].   [3] Rom. vii. [24].
[4] Psalm cxx. [5].   [5] Wisd. iii. [1—9]. v. [16].

now rejoice, who once were esteemed by the world as contemptible, and in a manner unworthy of life itself; truly thou wouldest forthwith humble thyself even to the earth, and wouldest rather seek to be under all, than to have command so much as over one.

Neither wouldest thou long for this life's pleasant days, but rather wouldst rejoice to suffer affliction for God, and esteem it thy greatest gain to be reputed as nothing amongst men.

IV. O if thou hadst a relishing of these things, and didst suffer them to sink into the bottom of thy heart, how couldest thou dare so much as once to complain?

Are not all painful labours to be endured for the sake of life eternal?

It is no small matter, to lose or to gain the Kingdom of God.

Lift up thy face therefore unto Heaven; behold, I and all My saints with Me, who in this world had great conflicts, do now rejoice, are now comforted, now secure, now at rest, and shall remain with Me everlastingly in the Kingdom of My Father.

CHAPTER XLVIII

OF THE DAY OF ETERNITY, AND THIS LIFE'S STRAITNESSES

O MOST blessed mansion of the City which is above![1] O most clear day of eternity, which night obscureth not, but the highest Truth ever enlighteneth! O day ever joyful, ever secure, and never changing into a contrary state!

O that that day might once appear, and that all these temporal things were at an end!

To the Saints indeed it shineth glowing with uninterrupted brightness, but to those who are pilgrims on

[1] Rev. xxi. [2].

the earth, it appeareth only afar off, and as through a glass.

II. The Citizens of Heaven do know how joyful that day is, but the banished children of Eve bewail the bitterness and tediousness of this.

The days of this life are few and evil,[1] full of sorrows and straitnesses.

Here a man is defiled with many sins, ensnared with many passions, held fast by many fears, racked with many cares, distracted with many curiosities, entangled with many vanities, compassed about with many errors, worn away with many labours, burdened with temptations, enervated by pleasures, tormented with want.

III. O when shall these evils be at an end? when shall I be delivered from the miserable bondage of my sins?[2] when shall I be mindful, O Lord, of Thee alone?[3] when shall I fully rejoice in Thee?

When shall I enjoy true liberty without all impediments whatsoever, without all trouble of mind and body?

When shall I have solid peace, peace secure and undisturbed, peace within and peace without, peace every way assured?

O merciful JESU, when shall I stand to behold Thee? when shall I contemplate the glory of Thy Kingdom? when wilt Thou be unto me all in all?

O when shall I be with Thee in Thy Kingdom, which Thou hast prepared for Thy beloved ones from all eternity?

I am left, a poor and banished man, in the land of mine enemies, where there are daily wars and very great calamities.

IV. Comfort my banishment, assuage my sorrow; for my whole desire sigheth after Thee.

For all is a burden to me, whatsoever this world offereth for consolation.

I long to enjoy Thee most inwardly, but I cannot attain unto it.

---

[1] Job vii.   [2] Rom. vii. [24].   [3] Psalm lxxi. [16].

My desire is, that I may be wholly given up to things heavenly, but temporal things and unmortified passions weigh me down.

With the mind I wish to be above all things, but with the flesh I am enforced against my will to be beneath them.

Thus, unhappy man that I am,[1] I fight against myself, and am become grievous to myself, whilst my spirit seeketh to be above, and my flesh to be below.

V. O what do I inwardly suffer, whilst in my mind I dwell on things Heavenly, and presently whilst I pray, a multitude of carnal temptations and thoughts occur to me ! O my God, be not Thou far from me, nor turn away in wrath from Thy servant.[2]

Cast forth Thy lightning, and disperse them ; shoot out Thine arrows, and let all the imaginations of the Enemy be confounded.

Gather in, and call home my senses unto Thee ; make me to forget all worldly things ; enable me to cast away speedily, and with scorn, all vicious imaginations.

Succour me, O Thou the everlasting Truth, that no vanity may move me.

Come to me, Thou heavenly sweetness, and let all impurity flee from before Thy face.

Pardon me also, and in mercy deal gently with me, as often as in prayer I think on aught beside Thee.

For truly I must confess, that I am wont to yield to many distractions.

Thus often and often it happens, that I am not where I am bodily standing or sitting, but rather there I am, whither my thoughts do carry me.

Where my thoughts are, there am I ; and commonly there are my thoughts, where my affection is.

That readily occurs to me, which naturally brings delight, or by custom is pleasing.

VI. And for this cause, Thou that art Truth itself hast plainly said, 'For where thy treasure is, there thy heart is also.'[3]

---

[1] Rom. vii. [24], viii. [23].   [2] Psalm lxxi. [12].
[3] Matt. vi. [21].

If I love Heaven, I willingly muse on Heavenly things.

If I love the world, I rejoice with the felicity of the world, and grieve for the adversity thereof.

If I love the flesh, I shall be constantly imagining those things that are pleasing to the flesh.

If I love the Spirit, I shall delight to think on things spiritual.

For whatsoever I love, thereof do I willingly speak and hear, and carry home with me the forms thereof.

But blessed is the man,[1] who for Thy sake, O Lord, is willing to part with all creatures, who does violence to his nature, and through fervour of the Spirit crucifieth the lust of the flesh; that so with a serene conscience he may offer pure prayers unto Thee, and all earthly things both outwardly and inwardly being excluded, he may be meet to be admitted into the Angelical choirs.

CHAPTER XLIX

OF THE DESIRE OF EVERLASTING LIFE, AND HOW GREAT REWARDS ARE PROMISED TO THOSE THAT STRIVE RESOLUTELY

MY son, when thou perceivest the desire of eternal bliss to be poured on thee from above, and longest to depart out of the tabernacle of the body, that thou mayest be able to contemplate My brightness, without shadow of turning; open thy heart wide, and receive this holy inspiration with thy whole desire.

Give greatest thanks to the Heavenly Goodness, which treateth thee with such condescension, visiting thee mercifully, stirring thee up fervently, sustaining thee

---

[1] Matt. xix. [12].

powerfully, lest through thine own weight thou sink down to earthly things.

For thou dost not obtain this by thy own thought or endeavour, but by the mere condescension of Heavenly grace and Divine regard ; to the end that thou mayest make further progress in all virtue, and in greater humility, and prepare thyself for future conflicts, earnestly striving to cleave unto Me with the whole affection of thy heart, and to serve Me with fervent willingness.

II. My son, oftentimes the fire burneth, but the flame ascendeth not up without smoke.

So likewise the desires of some men burn towards Heavenly things, and yet they are not free from temptation of carnal affection.

And therefore it is not altogether purely for the honour of God, that they make such earnest requests to Him.

Such also oftentimes are thy desires, which thou hast pretended to be so serious and earnest.

For those desires are not pure and perfect, which are tinctured with the love of thine own special interest and advantage.

III. Ask not for that which is delightful and profitable to thee, but for that which is acceptable to Me, and tends to My honour ; for if thou judgest aright, thou oughtest to prefer and follow My appointment, rather than thine own desire, or any thing whatever that is to be desired.

I know thy desire, and have oftentimes heard thy groanings.

Already thou longest to be in the glorious liberty of the sons of God ; already dost thou delight in the everlasting habitation, thy Heavenly home full of joy ; but that hour is not yet come; still there remaineth another time, and that a time of war,[1] a time of labour and of trial.

Thou desirest to be filled with the Chiefest Good, but thou canst not attain it just yet.

[1] Job vii. [1].

I AM He ; wait thou for Me (saith the Lord) until the Kingdom of God shall come.

IV. Thou art still to be tried upon earth, and to be exercised in many things.

Comfort shall be sometimes given thee, but the abundant fulness thereof shall not be granted.

Take courage therefore, and be valiant[1] as well in doing as in suffering things contrary to nature.

It is thy duty to put on the new Man,[2] and to be changed into another man.

It is thy duty oftentimes to do what thou wouldst not ; thy duty too to leave undone what thou wouldst do.

That which pleaseth others, shall go well forward ; that which pleaseth thee, shall not speed.

That which others say, shall be heard ; what thou sayest, shall be accounted nothing : Others shall ask and shall receive ; thou shalt ask but shalt not obtain.

V. Others shall be great in the praise of men, but about thee there shall be nothing said.

To others this or that shall be committed, but thou shalt be accounted of no use.

At this nature will sometimes be troubled, and it is a great thing if thou bear it with silence.

In these and many such like [things], the faithful servant of the Lord is wont to be tried, how far he can deny and break himself in all things.

There is scarcely any thing wherein thou hast such need to die to thyself, as in seeing and suffering those things that are adverse to thy will ; especially when that is commanded to be done, which seemeth unto thee inconvenient, or useless.

And because thou being under authority darest not resist the higher power, therefore it seems hard to thee to walk at another's beck, and to give up all thine own opinion.

VI. But consider, My son, the fruit of these labours, the end near at hand, and the reward exceeding great ;

---

[1] Joshua i. [7].   [2] Eph. iv. [24].

and thou wilt not grudge to bear them, rather thou wilt have the strongest comfort of thy patience.

For instead of that little of thy will, which now thou so readily forsakest, thou shalt always have thy will in Heaven.

There surely thou shalt find all that thou mayest wish, all that thou shalt be able to desire.

There thou shalt have within thy reach all good, without fear of losing it.

There shall thy will be ever one with Me; it shall not covet any outward or private thing.

There none shall withstand thee, no man shall complain of thee, no man hinder thee, nothing come in thy way; but all things thou canst desire shall be there together present, and refresh thy whole affection, and fill it up to the brim.

There I will give thee glory for the reproach which here thou sufferedst, the garment of praise for heaviness, for the lowest place a kingly throne for ever.

There shall the fruit of obedience appear, the labour of repentance shall rejoice, and humble subjection shall be gloriously crowned.

VII. At present then bend thyself humbly under all, and care not who said this or commanded it.

But take especial care, that whether thy superior, or thy inferior, or thine equal, require any thing of thee, or even insinuate their desire, thou take it all in good part, and with a sincere will endeavour to fulfil it.

Let one seek this, another that; let this man glory in this, the other in that, and be praised a thousand thousand times; but do thou rejoice neither in this, nor in that, but in the contempt of thyself, and in the good pleasure and honour of Me alone.

This is what thou art to wish, that whether it be by life or by death God may be always glorified in thee.

CHAPTER L

HOW A DESOLATE PERSON OUGHT TO OFFER HIMSELF INTO THE HANDS OF GOD

O LORD God, Holy Father, be Thou blessed both now and for evermore, because as Thou wilt, so is it done, and what Thou doest is good.

Let Thy servant rejoice in Thee, not in himself nor in any thing else ; for Thou alone art the true gladness, Thou art my hope and my crown, Thou art my joy and my honour, O Lord.

What hath Thy servant, but what he hath received from Thee,[1] even without any merit of his ?

Thine are all things, both what Thou hast given, and what Thou hast made.

I am poor, and in troubles, from my youth ;[2] and my soul is sorrowful sometimes even unto tears ; sometimes also my spirit is of itself disquieted, by reason of impending sufferings.

II. I long after the joy of Peace, the peace of Thy children I earnestly crave, who are fed by Thee in the light of Thy comfort.

If Thou give peace, if Thou pour into me holy joy, the soul of Thy servant shall be full of melody, and shall become devout in Thy praise.

But if Thou withdraw Thyself, (as too many times Thou dost,) he will not be able to run the way of Thy commandments ; but rather he will bow his knees, and smite his breast, because it is not now with him as it was in times past, when Thy candle shined upon his head, and under the shadow of Thy wings he was protected from the temptations which assaulted him.

III. O righteous Father, and ever to be praised, the hour is come that Thy servant is to be proved.

[1] 1 Cor. iv. [7].   [2] Psalm lxxxviii. [15].

O beloved Father, meet and right it is that in this hour Thy servant should suffer something for Thy sake.

O Father, evermore to be honoured, the hour is come, which from all eternity Thou didst foreknow should come ; that for a short time Thy servant should outwardly be oppressed, but inwardly should ever live with Thee

That he should be for a little while held despised, and humbled, and in the sight of men should fail, and be wasted with sufferings and languors ; that he may rise again with Thee in the morning dawn of the new Light, and be glorified in Heaven.

Holy Father, Thou hast so appointed it, and so wilt have it ; and that is fulfilled which Thyself hast commanded.

IV. For this is a favour to Thy friend, for Thy love to suffer and be afflicted in the world ; how often soever, and by whom soever, and in what way soever Thou permittest it to befall him.

Without Thy counsel and providence, and without cause, nothing cometh to pass in the earth.

It is good for me, Lord, that Thou hast humbled me,[1] that I may learn Thy righteous judgments, and may cast away all haughtiness of heart, and all presumptuousness.

It is profitable for me, that shame hath covered my face, that I may seek to Thee for consolation rather than to men.

I have learned also hereby to dread Thy unsearchable judgments, who afflictest the just with the wicked, though not without equity and justice.

V. I give Thee thanks, for that Thou hast not spared my sins, but hast worn me down with bitter stripes, inflicting sorrows and sending anxieties upon me within and without.

There is none else under Heaven who can comfort me, but Thou only, O Lord my God, the Heavenly

[1] Psalm cxix. [71].

Physician of souls, who strikest and healest, who bringest down to hell and bringest back again.[1]

Thy discipline over me, and Thy very rod itself shall instruct me.

VI. Behold, O beloved Father, I am in Thy hands, I bow myself under the rod of Thy correction.

Smite my back and my neck, that so I may bend my crookedness to Thy will.

Make me a dutiful and humble disciple, (as Thou art wont to be kind,) that I may be ever ready to go, if Thou dost but beckon to me.

Unto Thee I commend myself and all that is mine, to be corrected : better it is to be punished here, than hereafter.

Thou knowest all things generally, and also each separately, and there is nothing in man's conscience which can be hidden from Thee.

Before things are done, Thou knowest that they will come to pass ; and Thou hast no need that any should teach or admonish Thee of what is going on here on the earth.

Thou knowest what is expedient for my spiritual progress, and how greatly tribulation serves to scour off the rust of sins.

Do with me according to Thy desired good pleasure, and disdain me not for my sinful life, known to none so thoroughly and clearly as to Thee alone.

VII. Grant me, O Lord, to know that which is worth knowing, to love that which is worth loving, to praise that which pleaseth Thee most, to esteem that highly which to Thee is precious, to abhor that which in Thy sight is filthy and unclean.

Suffer me not to judge according to the sight of the outward eyes, nor to give sentence according to the hearing of the ears of ignorant men ; but with a true judgment to discern between things visible and spiritual, and above all to be ever searching after the good pleasure of Thy will.

---

[1] Tob. xiii. [2] ; Psalm xviii. [16].

VIII. The minds of men are often deceived in their judgments; the lovers of the world too are deceived in loving only things visible.

What is a man ever the better, for being by man esteemed great?

The deceitful in flattering the deceitful, the vain man in extolling the vain, the blind in commending the blind, the weak in magnifying the weak, deceiveth him; and in truth doth rather put him to shame, while he so vainly praiseth him.

'For what every one is in Thy sight, that is he, and no more,' saith humble St. Francis.

CHAPTER LI

THAT A MAN OUGHT TO EMPLOY HIMSELF IN WORKS OF HUMILITY, WHEN STRENGTH IS WANTING FOR HIGHER EMPLOYMENTS

My son, thou art not able always to continue in the more fervent desire of all that is virtuous, nor to persist in the higher pitch of contemplation; but thou must needs sometimes by reason of original corruption descend to inferior things, and bear the burden of this corruptible life, though against thy will, and with wearisomeness.

As long as thou carriest a mortal body, thou shalt feel weariness and heaviness of heart.

Thou oughtest therefore in the flesh oftentimes to bewail the burden of the flesh; for that thou canst not employ thyself unceasingly in spiritual studies and divine contemplation.

II. Then it is expedient for thee to flee to humble and exterior works, and to refresh thyself with good actions; to expect with a firm confidence My coming and Heavenly visitation; to bear patiently thy banishment and the dryness of thy mind, till I shall again visit thee, and set thee free from all anxieties.

For I will cause thee to forget thy painful toils, and to enjoy thorough inward quietness.

I will spread open before thee the pleasant fields of the Scriptures, that with an enlarged heart thou mayest begin to run the way of My commandments.

And thou shalt say, 'The sufferings of this present time are not worthy to be compared with the future glory, that shall be revealed in us.'[1]

CHAPTER LII

THAT A MAN OUGHT NOT TO ACCOUNT HIMSELF AS WORTHY OF COMFORT, BUT RATHER AS DESERVING OF CHASTISEMENT

O LORD, I am not worthy of Thy consolation, nor of any spiritual visitations; and therefore Thou dealest justly with me, when Thou leavest me poor and desolate.

For though I could shed a sea of tears, still I should not be worthy of Thy consolation.

I am not then worthy of any thing but to be scourged and punished; because grievously and often I have offended Thee, and in many things have greatly sinned.

Wherefore, in the judgment of truth and reason, I am not worthy even of the least comfort.

But Thou, O gracious and merciful God, who willest not that Thy works should perish, to shew the riches of Thy goodness upon the vessels of mercy, vouchsafest even beyond all his desert to comfort Thy servant above the manner of men.

For Thy consolations are not like to the discourses of men.

II. What have I done, O Lord, that thou shouldest bestow any heavenly comfort upon me?

I remember not that I have done any good, but that I have been always prone to sin, and slow to amendment.

[1] Rom. viii. [18].

This is true, and I cannot deny it. If I should say otherwise, Thou wouldest stand against me;[1] and there would be none to defend me.

What have I deserved for my sins, but hell and everlasting fire?

I confess in very truth that I am worthy of all scorn and contempt, nor is it fit that I should be remembered amongst Thy devout servants.

And although I be unwilling to hear this, yet notwithstanding, I will for the Truth's sake lay open my sins, even against myself, that so the more readily I may be accounted worthy to obtain Thy mercy.

III. What shall I say, in that I am guilty, and full of all confusion?

My mouth can utter nothing but this word only, 'I have sinned, O Lord! I have sinned;[2] have mercy on me, pardon me!'

Suffer me a little, that I may bewail my griefs, before I go into the land of darkness, a land covered with the shadow of death.[3]

What dost Thou so much require of a guilty and miserable sinner, as that he be contrite, and that he humble himself for his offences?

Of true contrition and humbling of the heart, ariseth hope of forgiveness; the troubled conscience is reconciled; the grace which was lost, is recovered; man is preserved from the wrath to come; and God and the penitent soul meet together with a holy kiss.

IV. Humble contrition for sins is an acceptable sacrifice unto Thee, O Lord,[4] giving forth a savour far sweeter in Thy sight than the perfume of frankincense.

This is also the pleasant ointment,[5] which Thou wouldest should be poured upon Thy sacred feet; for a contrite and humble heart Thou never hast despised.[6]

Here is the place of refuge from the angry face of

---

[1] Job ix. [2, 3]. [2] Psalm li. [3] Job x. [21].
[4] Psalm li. [17]. [5] Luke vii. [38]. [6] Psalm li. [17].

the Enemy; here is amended and washed away whatever defilement and pollution hath been any where else contracted.

CHAPTER LIII

THAT THE GRACE OF GOD DOTH NOT JOIN ITSELF WITH THOSE WHO RELISH EARTHLY THINGS

My son, My grace is precious, it suffereth not itself to be mingled with external things, nor with earthly consolations.

Thou oughtest therefore to cast away the hindrances of Grace, if thou desire to receive the infusion thereof.

Look out for a secret place for thyself, love to dwell alone with thyself, desire the conversation of none; but rather pour out devout prayer unto God, that thou mayest keep thy mind in compunction, and thy conscience pure.

Esteem thou the whole world as nothing; prefer attendance upon God before all outward things.

For thou wilt not be able to attend upon Me, and at the same time to take delight in things transitory.

It is meet that thou remove thyself far away from acquaintance and dear friends,[1] and keep thy mind void of all temporal comfort.

So the blessed Apostle Peter beseecheth, that the faithful of Christ would keep themselves in this world as strangers and pilgrims.[2]

II. O how great a confidence shall we have at the hour of death, whom no affection to any thing detaineth in the world.

But what it is to have a heart so alienated from all things, the sickly mind doth not as yet comprehend;

[1] Matt. xix. [29].   [2] 1 Pet. ii. [11].

nor doth the carnal man know the liberty of the spiritual man.

Notwithstanding if he would be truly spiritual, he ought to renounce as well those who are far off, as those who are near unto him, and to beware of no man more than of himself.

If thou perfectly overcome thyself, thou shalt very easily bring all else under the yoke.

The perfect victory is, to triumph over ourselves.

For he that keepeth himself subject, in such sort that his sensual affections be obedient to reason, and his reason in all things obedient to Me; that person is truly conqueror of himself, and lord of the world.

III. If thou desire to mount unto this height, thou must set out courageously, and lay the axe to the root, that thou mayest pluck up and destroy the hidden inordinate inclination to self, and all love of private and earthly good.

By this vicious propensity (namely, man's too inordinate love of self) every thing almost is upheld, which ought thoroughly to be overcome. If this evil be once vanquished and subdued, there will presently ensue great peace and tranquillity.

But because few labour to be perfectly dead to themselves, or fully go forth from themselves, therefore in themselves they remain entangled, nor can be lifted up in spirit above themselves.

But he that desireth to walk freely with Me, it is necessary that he mortify all his corrupt and inordinate affections, and that he should not earnestly cleave to any creature with particular love.

CHAPTER LIV

OF THE DIFFERENT MOTIONS OF NATURE AND GRACE

My son, mark diligently the motions of Nature and of Grace; for in a very contrary and subtle manner do they move, and can hardly be distinguished but by him that is spiritually and inwardly enlightened.

All men indeed desire that which is good, and pretend somewhat good in their words and deeds; and therefore under the show of good, many are deceived.

Nature is crafty, and seduceth many, ensnareth and deceiveth them, and hath always self for her end and object:

But Grace walketh in simplicity, abstaineth from all show of evil, sheltereth not herself under deceits, doeth all things purely for God's sake, in whom also she finally resteth.

II. Nature is reluctant and loth to die, or to be kept down, or to be overcome, or to be in subjection, or readily to be subdued:

But Grace studieth self-mortification, resisteth sensuality, seeketh to be in subjection, longeth to be defeated, hath no wish to use her own liberty; she loves to be kept under discipline, and desires not to rule over any, but always to live, remain, and be under God, and for God's sake is ready humbly to bow down to every ordinance of man.

Nature striveth for her own advantage, and considereth what profit she may reap by another:

Grace considereth not what is profitable and commodious unto herself, but rather what may be for the good of many.

Nature willingly receiveth honour and reverence:

But Grace faithfully attributeth all honour and glory unto God.

III. Nature feareth shame and contempt:

But Grace rejoiceth to suffer reproach for the Name of JESUS.

Nature loveth leisure and bodily rest :

Grace cannot be unemployed, but cheerfully embraceth labour.

Nature seeketh to have things that are curious and beautiful, and abhorreth those which are cheap and coarse :

But Grace delighteth in what is plain and humble, despiseth not rough things, nor refuseth to wear that which is old and patched.

Nature respecteth temporal things, rejoiceth at earthly gains, sorroweth for loss, is irritated by every little injurious word :

But Grace looks to things eternal, cleaves not to things temporal, is not disturbed at losses, nor soured with hard words ; because she hath placed her treasure and joy in Heaven, where nothing perisheth.

IV. Nature is covetous, doth more willingly receive than give, and loveth to have things private and her own :

But Grace is kind-hearted and communicative, shunneth private interest, is content with a little, judgeth that it is more blessed to give than to receive.

Nature inclines a man to the creatures, to his own flesh, to vanities, and to vagaries hither and thither :

But Grace draweth unto God and to every virtue, renounceth creatures, avoideth the world, hateth the desires of the flesh, restraineth wanderings abroad, blusheth to be seen in public.

Nature is willing to have some outward solace, wherein she may be sensibly delighted :

But Grace secketh consolation in God alone, and to have delight in the highest Good above all visible things.

V. Nature manages every thing for her own gain and profit, she cannot bear to do any thing *gratis*, but for every kindness she hopes to obtain either what is equal, or what is better, or at least praise or favour ;

and is very earnest to have her works and gifts and words much valued :

But Grace seeketh no temporal thing, nor desireth any other reward than God alone, nor asketh more of temporal necessaries, than what may serve her for the obtaining of things eternal.

VI. Nature rejoiceth to have many friends and kins-folk, she glorieth of noble place and noble birth, smiles on the powerful, fawns upon the rich, applauds those who are like herself :

But Grace loves even her enemies, and is not puffed up with multitude of friends ; nor thinks aught of high birth, unless it be joined with more exalted virtue :

She favoureth the poor rather than the rich, sym-pathiseth more with the innocent than with the powerful, rejoiceth with the true man, not with the deceitful :

She is ever exhorting good men to strive for the best gifts ; and by all virtue to become like to the Son of God.

Nature quickly complaineth of want and of trouble :

Grace endureth need with firmness and constancy.

VII. Nature referreth all things to herself, striveth and argueth for herself :

But Grace bringeth back all to God, from whence originally they proceed ; she ascribeth no good to herself, nor doth she arrogantly presume ; she con-tendeth not, nor preferreth her own opinion before others ; but in every matter of sense and understanding submitteth herself unto the Eternal wisdom and the Divine judgment.

Nature is eager to know secrets, and to hear news ; she likes to appear abroad, and to make proof of many things by her own senses ; she desires to be acknow-ledged, and do things for which she may be praised and admired :

But Grace cares not to hear news, nor to understand curious matters, (because all this takes its rise from the old corruption of man,) seeing that upon earth there is nothing new, nothing durable.

Grace teacheth therefore to restrain the senses, to

shun vain complacency and ostentation, humbly to hide those things that are worthy of admiration and praise, and from every matter and in every knowledge to seek profitable fruit, and the praise and honour of God.

She will not have herself nor hers publicly praised, but desireth that God should be blessed in His gifts, who of mere love bestoweth all things.

VIII. This Grace is a supernatural light, and a certain special gift of God, and the proper mark of the Elect, and pledge of everlasting salvation ; it raiseth up a man from earthly things to love the things of Heaven, and from being carnal maketh him a spiritual man.

The more therefore Nature is depressed and subdued, so much the greater Grace is infused, and every day by new visitations the inward man becomes reformed according to the image of God.

CHAPTER LV

OF THE CORRUPTION OF NATURE, AND EFFICACY OF DIVINE GRACE

O Lord my God, who hast created me after Thine own image and likeness,[1] grant me this Grace, which Thou hast shewed to be so great and so necessary to salvation ; that I may overcome my most evil nature, which draweth me to sin and to perdition.

For I feel in my flesh the law of sin contradicting the law of my mind,[2] and leading me captive to the obeying of sensuality in many things ; neither can I resist the passions thereof, unless Thy most holy Grace fervently infused into my heart do assist me.

II. There is need of Thy Grace, O Lord, and of great degrees thereof, that Nature may be overcome, which is ever prone to evil from her youth.[3]

---

[1] Gen. i. [26].   [2] Rom. vii. [23].   [3] Gen. viii. [21].

For through Adam the first man, Nature being fallen
and corrupted by sin, the penalty of this stain hath
descended upon all mankind, in such sort, that 'Nature'
itself, which by Thee was created good and upright,
is now taken for the sin and infirmity of corrupted
nature ; because the inclination thereof left unto itself
draweth to evil and to inferior things.

For the small power which remaineth is as it were
a spark lying hid in the ashes.

This is Natural Reason itself, encompassed about with
great darkness, yet still retaining power to discern the
difference between good and evil, true and false,
although it be unable to fulfil all that it approveth,
and enjoyeth no longer the full light of the Truth, nor
soundness of its own affections.

III. Hence it is, O my God, that I delight in Thy
law after the inward man,[1] knowing Thy commandment
to be good, just and holy, reproving also all evil and
sin, as things to be avoided.

But with the flesh I serve the law of sin, whilst I obey
sensuality rather than reason.

Hence it is, that to will what is good is present with
me, but how to perform it I find not.

Hence it is that I often purpose many good things,
but because Grace is wanting to help my infirmity, upon
a light resistance I start back and faint.

Hence it comes to pass that I know the way of perfection, and see clearly enough how I ought to act ;
but being pressed down with the weight of mine own
corruption, I rise not to what is more perfect.

IV. O Lord, how entirely needful is Thy Grace for
me, to begin any thing good, to proceed with it, and to
accomplish it.

For without it I can do nothing.[2] but in Thee I can
do all things, when Thy Grace doth strengthen me.

O Grace truly celestial ! without which our most
worthy actions are nothing, nor are any gifts of nature
to be esteemed.

---

[1] Rom. vii. [22].   [2] John xv. [5].

Neither arts or riches, beauty or strength, wit or eloquence, are of any value before Thee, without Thy Grace, O Lord.

For gifts of nature are common to good and bad, but the peculiar gift of the elect is Grace and Love; and they that bear this honourable mark, are accounted worthy of everlasting life.

So eminent is this Grace that neither the gift of prophecy, nor the working of miracles, nor any speculation (how high soever) is of any esteem without it.

No, not even faith or hope, or any other virtues, are unto Thee acceptable without Charity and Grace.[1]

V. O most blessed grace, that makest the poor in spirit rich in virtues, and renderest him who is rich in many goods humble in heart!

Come Thou down unto me, come and replenish me early with Thy comfort, lest my soul faint for weariness and dryness of mind.

I beseech Thee, O Lord, that I may find Grace in Thy sight; for Thy Grace is sufficient for me, though other things that Nature longeth for be not obtained.

Although I be tempted and vexed with many tribulations, yet I will fear no evils,[2] so long as Thy Grace is with me.

This alone and by itself is my strength; this alone giveth advice and help.

This is stronger than all enemies, and wiser than all the wise.

VI. Thy Grace is the mistress of truth, the teacher of discipline, the light of the heart, the solace in affliction, the driver away of sorrow, the expeller of fear, the nurse of devotion, the source and fountain of tears.

Without this, what am I but a withered piece of wood, and an unprofitable branch only meet to be cast away.

---

[1] 1 Cor. xiii. [13].　　　　[2] Psalm xxiii. [4].

Let Thy grace therefore, O Lord, always prevent and follow me, and make me to be continually given to good works, through Thy Son Jesus Christ. Amen.

CHAPTER LVI

THAT WE OUGHT TO DENY OURSELVES AND IMITATE CHRIST BY THE CROSS

My son, the more thou canst go out of thyself, so much the more wilt thou be able to enter into Me.

As to be void of all desire of external things, produceth inward peace, so the forsaking of thyself inwardly, joineth thee unto God.

I wish thee to learn perfect resignation of thyself to My will, without contradiction or complaint.

Follow thou Me : 'I am the Way, the Truth, and the Life.'[1] Without the Way, there is no going; without the Truth, there is no knowing; without the Life, there is no living. I am the Way, which thou oughtest to follow ; the Truth, which thou oughtest to trust ; the Life, which thou oughtest to hope for.

I am the inviolable Way, the infallible Truth, the endless Life.

I am the straightest Way, the supreme Truth, the true, the blessed, the uncreated Life.

If thou remain in My way, thou shalt know the Truth, and the Truth shall make thee free, and thou shalt lay hold on eternal Life.

II. If thou wilt enter into life, keep the commandments.[2]

If thou wilt know the truth, believe Me.

If thou wilt be perfect, sell all.[3]

If thou wilt be My disciple, deny thyself utterly.[4]

---

[1] John xiv. [6].
[2] Matt. xix. [17].
[3] Matt. xix. [21].
[4] Luke ix. [23].

If thou wilt possess a blessed life, despise this life present.

If thou wilt be exalted in Heaven, humble thyself in this world.[1]

If thou wilt reign with Me, bear the Cross with Me.[2]

For only the servants of the Cross do find the way of blessedness and of true light.

III. O LORD JESUS, forasmuch as Thy life was strict and despised by the world, grant me grace to imitate Thee, though with the world's contempt.

For the servant is not greater than his Lord,[3] nor the disciple above his Master.

Let Thy servant be exercised in Thy life, for therein my salvation and true holiness doth consist.

Whatsoever I read or hear besides it, doth not give me full refreshment or delight.

IV. My son, inasmuch as thou knowest and hast read all these things, happy shalt thou be, if thou do them.

'He that hath My commandments and keepeth them, he it is that loveth Me; and I will love him, and will manifest Myself unto him,'[4] and will make him sit together with Me in My Father's kingdom.

O LORD JESU, as Thou hast said and promised, so truly let it come to pass, and grant that I may not be wholly undeserving of this favour.

I have received the Cross, I have received it from Thy hand; I will bear it, and bear it even unto death, as Thou hast laid it upon me.

Truly the life of a good Christian is a Cross, yet it is also a guide to Paradise.

We have now begun, it is not lawful to go back, neither is it fit to leave that which we have undertaken.

---

[1] John xii. [25].   [2] Luke xiv. [27].
[3] Matt. x. [24]; Luke vi. [40].   [4] John xiv. [21].

V. Let us then take courage, brethren, let us go forward together, Jesus will be with us.

For the sake of Jesus we have undertaken this Cross; for the sake of Jesus let us persevere in the Cross.

He will be our Helper, who is also our Guide and Forerunner.

Behold, our King entereth in before us, and He will fight for us.

Let us follow manfully, let no man fear any terrors: let us be prepared to die valiantly in battle, nor bring such a disgrace on our glory as to flee from the Cross.

CHAPTER LVII

THAT A MAN SHOULD NOT BE TOO MUCH DEJECTED, EVEN WHEN HE FALLETH INTO SOME DEFECTS

My son, patience and humility in adversities are more pleasing to Me, than much comfort and devotion when things go well.

Why art thou so grieved for every little matter spoken against thee?

Although it had been much more, thou oughtest not to have been moved.

But now let it pass; it is not the first that hath happened, nor is it any thing new; neither shall it be the last, if thou live long.

Thou art courageous enough, so long as nothing adverse befalleth thee.

Thou canst give good counsel also, and canst strengthen others with thy words; but when any tribulation suddenly comes to thy door, thou failest in counsel and in strength.

Observe then thy great frailty, of which thou too often hast experience in small occurrences.

It is notwithstanding intended for thy good, when these and such like trials happen to thee.

II. Put it out of thy heart the best thou canst, and if tribulation have touched thee, yet let it not cast thee down, nor long perplex thee.

Bear it at least patiently, if thou canst not joyfully.

Although thou be unwilling to hear it, and conceivest indignation thereat, yet restrain thyself, and suffer no inordinate word to pass out of thy mouth, whereby Christ's little ones may be offended.

The storm which is now raised shall quickly be appeased, and inward grief shall be sweetened by the return of Grace.

I yet live, saith the Lord, and am ready to help thee,[1] and to give thee more than ordinary consolation, if thou put thy trust in Me, and call devoutly upon Me.

III. Be more patient of soul, and gird thyself to greater endurance.

All is not lost, although thou do feel thyself very often afflicted or grievously tempted.

Thou art a man, and not God; thou art flesh, not an Angel.

How canst thou look to continue alway in the same state of virtue, when an Angel in Heaven hath fallen, as also the first man in Paradise?[2]

I am He who lift up the mourners to safety and soundness, and those that know their own weakness I advance to My own Divine [Nature].

IV. O Lord, blessed be Thy Word, more sweet unto my mouth than honey and the honey-comb.[3]

What should I do in these so great tribulations and straits, unless Thou didst comfort me with Thy holy discourses?

What matter is it, how much or what I suffer, so as I may at length attain to the port of salvation?

[1] Isaiah xlix.   [2] Gen. iii.   [3] Psalm cxix. [103].

Grant me a good end, grant me a happy passage out of this world.

Be mindful of me, O my God, and direct me in the right way of Thy kingdom.   Amen.

CHAPTER LVIII

THAT HIGH MATTERS AND GOD'S SECRET JUDGMENTS ARE NOT TO BE NARROWLY ENQUIRED INTO

My son, beware thou dispute not of high matters, nor of the secret judgments of God, why this man is so left, and that man taken into such great favour; why also one is so grievously afflicted, and another so eminently exalted.

These things are beyond all reach of man's faculties, neither is it in the power of any reason or disputation to search out the judgments of God.

When therefore the Enemy suggesteth these things unto thee, or some curious people raise the question, let thy answer be that of the Prophet, 'Thou art just, O Lord, and Thy judgment is right.'[1]

And again, 'The judgments of the Lord are true and righteous altogether.'[2]

My judgments are to be feared, not to be discussed; for they are such as cannot be comprehended by the understanding of man.

II. In like manner I advise thee not to enquire, nor dispute of the merits of holy men as to which of them is holier than the other, or which shall be the greater in the kingdom of Heaven.

Such matters oftentimes breed unprofitable strifes and contentions,[3] they also nourish pride and vainglory; whence arise envies and dissensions, whilst one

[1] Psalm cxix. [137].   [2] Psalm xix. [9].
[3] 2 Tim. ii. [14].

proudly endeavours to put forward one saint, and the other another.

To wish to know and search out such things answers no good end, rather is displeasing to the righteous Souls ; for I am not the God of dissension, but of peace ; which peace consisteth rather in true humility, than in self-exaltation.

III. Some are carried with zeal of affection towards these Saints or those ; nevertheless this is rather human love than divine.

I am He who made all the Saints ; I gave them Grace ; I obtain for them Glory.

I know what every one hath deserved ; I have prevented them with the blessings of My goodness.

I foreknew My beloved ones before the beginning of the world.

I chose them out of the world, they chose not Me first.[1]

I called them by grace, I drew them by mercy, I led them safe through sundry temptations.

I poured into them glorious consolations, I gave them perseverance, I crowned their patience.

IV. I acknowledge both the first and the last ; I embrace all with love inestimable.

I am to be praised in all My Saints ; I am to be blessed above all things, and to be honoured in every one, whom I have thus gloriously exalted and predestinated, without any precedent merits of their own.

He therefore that contemneth one of the least of Mine,[2] honoureth not the greatest ; for that I made both the small and the great.[3]

And he that disparageth any of the Saints, disparageth Me also, and all other in the Kingdom of Heaven.

These all are one through the bond of charity ; their thought is the same, their will is the same, and in love they are all united one to another.

V. But still, (which is a far higher consideration,)

---

[1] John xv. [16].   [2] James ii. [1—5].   [3] Wisdom vi. [7].

they love Me more than they do themselves **or any**
merits of their own.

For being ravished above self and self-love, they are
wholly carried out to love Me, in whom also they rest
with entire fruition.

Nothing can turn them back, nothing can press them
down ; for being full of the eternal Truth, they burn
with the fire of unquenchable charity.

Let therefore carnal and natural men who can love
nothing but their own selfish joys, forbear to dispute
of the state of God's Saints.   Such men add and take
away according to their own fancies, not as it pleaseth
the eternal Truth.

VI. Many are ignorant, especially those who being
but slenderly enlightened, can seldom love any with a
perfect spiritual love.

They are as yet much drawn by natural affection and
human friendship to this man or to that ; and according
to the experience they have of themselves in their
earthly affections, so do they frame imaginations of
things heavenly.

But there is an incomparable distance between the
things which the imperfect imagine in their conceits,
and those which the illuminated are enabled to behold,
through revelation from above.

VII. Beware, therefore, My son, that thou handle
not with vain curiosity things which exceed thy
knowledge ;[1] but rather let this be thy great business
and endeavour, to attain if it be the meanest place in
the kingdom of God.

Even if any man should know who exceeds another
in sanctity, or who is accounted the greatest in the
kingdom of Heaven ; what would this wisdom profit
him, unless he should humble himself the more in My
sight, and then should rise up to give the greater
praise to My Name, in proportion to this his knowledge ?

Far more acceptable to God is he that thinketh of

---

[1] Ecclus. iii. [21].

the greatness of his own sins, and the smallness of his virtues, and how far he is from the perfection of Saints, than he who disputeth of their greatness or littleness.

VIII. They are well yea right well contented, if men would but content themselves, and refrain from their vain discourses.

They glory not of their own merits, inasmuch as they ascribe no goodness to themselves, but attribute all to Me, who of My infinite love have given them all things.

They are filled with so great love of the Divinity, and with such an overflowing joy, that there is no glory nor happiness that is or can be wanting unto them.

All the Saints, the higher they are in glory, so much the more humble are they in themselves, and the nearer and dearer unto Me.

And therefore thou hast it written, 'That they did cast their crowns before God, and fell down on their faces before the Lamb, and adored Him that liveth for ever and ever.' [1]

IX. Many enquire, who is the greatest in the kingdom of God, who know not whether they shall ever be numbered among the least.

It is a great thing to be even the least in Heaven, where all are great; for they all shall be called, and shall be, the Sons of God.

'The least shall become a thousand,' [2] and 'the sinner of an hundred years shall die.' [3]

For when the disciples asked who should be greatest in the kingdom of Heaven, they received such an answer as this:

'Except ye be converted, and become as little children, ye shall not enter into the kingdom of Heaven; whosoever therefore shall humble himself as this little child, the same is greatest in the kingdom of Heaven.' [4]

X. Woe be unto them who disdain to humble them-

---

[1] Rev. iv. [10].   [2] [Isaiah lx. 22.]
[3] [Isaiah lxv. 20.]   [4] Matt. xviii. [3].

selves willingly with little children ; because the low gate of the kingdom of Heaven will not give them entrance.[1]

Woe also to the rich, who have here their consolation ; for whilst the poor enter into the kingdom of God, they shall stand lamenting without.

Rejoice ye that be humble,[2] and ye poor be ye filled with joy, for yours is the kingdom of God, if at least ye walk according to the Truth.

CHAPTER LIX

THAT ALL OUR HOPE AND TRUST IS TO BE FIXED IN GOD ALONE

LORD, what is my confidence which I have in this life? or what is the greatest comfort I can derive from any thing under Heaven ?

Is it not Thou, O Lord my God, whose mercies are without number ?

Where hath it ever been well with me without Thee ? or when could it be ill with me, when Thou wert present ?

I had rather be poor for Thee, than rich without Thee.

I rather choose to be a pilgrim on earth with Thee, than without Thee to possess Heaven.   Where Thou art, there is Heaven : and where Thou art not, there is death and hell.

Thou art all my desire, and therefore I must needs sigh and call and earnestly pray unto Thee.

In short there is none whom I can fully trust to, none that can seasonably help me in my necessities, but only Thou, my God.

---

[1] Matt. vii. [11].   [2] Matt. v. [3].

Thou art my hope, Thou my confidence ; Thou art my Comforter, and in all things most faithful unto Me.

II. All men seek their own gain ;[1] Thou settest forward my salvation and my profit only, and turnest all things to my good.

Although Thou exposest me to divers temptations and adversities, yet Thou orderest all this to my advantage, who art wont to try Thy beloved ones a thousand ways.

In which trial of me Thou oughtest no less to be loved and praised, than if Thou didst fill me full of heavenly consolations.

III. In Thee therefore, O Lord God, I place my whole hope and refuge ; on Thee I rest all my tribulation and anguish ; for I find all to be weak and inconstant, whatsoever I behold out of Thee.

For many friends cannot profit, nor strong helpers assist, nor prudent counsellors give a profitable answer, nor the books of the learned afford comfort, nor any precious substance deliver, nor any place, however retired and lovely, give shelter, unless Thou Thyself dost assist, help, strengthen, console, instruct, and guard us.

IV. For all things that seem to belong to the attainment of peace and felicity, without Thee, are nothing, and do bring in truth no felicity at all.

Thou therefore art the Fountain of all that is good, the Height of life, the Depth of all that can be spoken ; and to hope in Thee above all things, is the strongest comfort of Thy servants.

To Thee therefore do I lift up mine eyes ; in Thee my God, the Father of mercies, do I put my trust.

Bless and sanctify my soul with Thy heavenly blessings, that it may become Thy holy habitation, and the seat of Thine eternal glory ; and let nothing be found in this temple of Thy Divinity, which shall offend the eyes of Thy Majesty.

[1] Phil. ii. [21.]

According to the greatness of Thy goodness and multitude of Thy mercies look upon me, and hear the prayer of Thy poor servant, who is far exiled from Thee in the land of the shadow of death.

Protect and keep the soul of me the meanest of Thy servants, amidst so many dangers of this corruptible life, and by Thy grace accompanying me direct it along the way of peace to its home of everlasting brightness. Amen.

THE FOURTH BOOK

CONCERNING THE SACRAMENT

A DEVOUT EXHORTATION TO THE HOLY COMMUNION

The Voice of Christ.

'Come unto Me all ye that labour and are heavy laden, and I will refresh you,'[1] saith the Lord.

'The bread which I will give is My Flesh, for the life of the world.'[2]

'Take ye and eat; this is My Body which is given for you:[3] Do this in remembrance of Me.'[4]

'He that eateth My Flesh and drinketh My Blood, dwelleth in Me, and I in him.'

'The Words which I have spoken unto you are Spirit and Life.'[5]

CHAPTER I

WITH HOW GREAT REVERENCE CHRIST OUGHT TO BE RECEIVED

The Voice of the Disciple.

THESE are Thy words, O Christ the everlasting Truth, though not uttered all at one time, nor written in one and the self-same place.

---

[1] Matt. xi. [28]. [2] John vi. [51]. [3] Matt. xxvi. [26].
[4] 1 Cor. xi. [24]. [5] John vi. [56, 63].

Because therefore they are Thine and true, they are all thankfully and faithfully to be received by me.

They are Thine, and Thou hast pronounced them; and they are mine also, because Thou hast spoken them for my salvation.

I cheerfully receive them from Thy mouth, that they may be the more deeply implanted in my heart.

They arouse me, those most gracious words so full of sweetness and of love; but mine own offences do dishearten me, and an impure conscience driveth me back from the receiving of so great Mysteries.

The sweetness of Thy words doth encourage me, but the multitude of my sins weigheth me down.

II. Thou commandest me to come confidently unto Thee, if I would have part with Thee; and to receive the food of immortality, if I desire to obtain everlasting life and glory.

'Come unto Me, (sayest Thou,) all ye that labour and are heavy laden, and I will refresh you.'[1]

O sweet and loving word in the ear of a sinner, that Thou, my Lord God, shouldest invite the poor and needy to the participation of Thy most holy Body and Blood!

But who am I, Lord, that I should presume to approach unto Thee?

Behold the Heaven of Heavens cannot contain Thee, and Thou sayest, 'Come ye all unto Me.'

III. What meaneth this so gracious a condescension, and this so loving invitation?

How shall I dare to come, who know not any good in myself, whereupon I may presume!

How shall I bring Thee into my house, I that have so often offended Thy most benign countenance?

Angels and Archangels stand in awe of Thee, holy and righteous men do fear Thee, and sayest Thou, 'Come ye all unto Me?'

Unless Thou, O Lord, didst say this, who would believe it to be true?

---

[1] Matt. xi. [28].

And unless Thou didst command it, who could attempt to draw near?

Behold, Noah that just man laboured a hundred years in the making of the Ark,[1] that he might be saved with a few ; and how can I in one hour's space prepare myself to receive with reverence the Maker of the world?

IV. Moses, Thy great servant, and Thine especial friend, made an ark of incorruptible wood, which also he covered over with the finest gold, wherein to lay up the tables of the law ;[2] and I a corrupted creature, how shall I dare so unconcernedly to receive the Maker of the Law, and the Giver of life?

Solomon the wisest of the kings of Israel bestowed seven years in building a magnificent Temple to the praise of Thy Name.[3]

He also celebrated the feast of dedication thereof for eight days together ; he offered a thousand peace-offerings, and he solemnly set the Ark of the Covenant in the place prepared for it, with the sound of trumpets, and great joy.[4]

And I the most miserable and poorest of men, how shall I bring Thee into my house, I that can scarce spend one half-hour in true devotion? and would that I could even once spend something like one half-hour in worthy and due manner !

V. O my God, how earnestly did they study and endeavour to please Thee !

Alas, how little is that which I do ! how short a time do I spend, when I am disposing myself to receive the Communion !

Seldom am I wholly collected ; very seldom indeed am I cleansed from all distraction.

And yet surely in the life-giving Presence of Thy Godhead no unbecoming thought ought to intrude itself, nor should any creature occupy my heart ; for it is not an Angel, but the Lord of the Angels, whom I am about to receive as my Guest.

[1] Gen. vi. [3].   [2] Exod. xxv. [10—16].
[3] 1 Kings vi. [38].   [4] 2 Kings viii.

VI. However, very great is the difference between the ark of the covenant with its relicks, and Thy most pure Body with Its unspeakable virtues ; between those legal sacrifices, figures of things to come, and the True Sacrifice of Thy Body, the fulfilment of all ancient sacrifices.

Wherefore then am I not more ardent and zealous in seeking Thine adorable Presence?

Why do I not prepare myself with greater solicitude to receive Thy holy things? whereas those ancient holy patriarchs and prophets, yea kings also and princes, with the whole people, shewed such an affectionateness of devotion to Thy divine service.

VII. The most devout King David[1] danced before the ark of God with all his might, calling to mind the benefits bestowed in time past upon his forefathers. He made instruments of sundry kinds, he published psalms, and appointed them to be chanted with joy ; he also oftentimes himself played on the harp, being inspired with the grace of the Holy Ghost. He taught the people of Israel to praise God with their whole hearts, and with voices full of melody to bless and praise Him every day.

If so great devotion was then used, and such celebrating of divine praise was kept up before the ark of the testament ; what reverence and devotion ought now to be preserved by me and all Christian people during the ministration of the Sacrament, in receiving the most precious Body and Blood of Christ.

VIII. Many run to divers places to visit the memorials of Saints departed, are full of admiration at hearing of their deeds, behold with awe the spacious buildings of their temples, and find their affections moved by whatever is connected with their memory.

But behold, Thou art Thyself here present with me on Thine altar, my God, Saint of saints, Creator of men, and Lord of the Angels.

Often in looking after such memorials people are

---

[1] 2 Sam. vi. [14 ; Ecclus. xlvii. 8, 9].

moved by curiosity, and the novelty of fresh sights, whilst little or no fruit of amendment is carried home ; particularly when they go from place to place with such levity, without true contrition of heart.

But here, in the Sacrament of the Altar, Thou art wholly present, my God, The Man Christ JESUS ; here, to all worthy and devout receivers, is granted an abundant fruit of eternal salvation.

There is here to attract men nothing that savours of levity, of curiosity, or of sensuality ; nothing but firm faith, devout hope, and sincere charity.

IX. O God, the invisible Creator of the world, how wonderfully dost Thou deal with us ; how sweetly and graciously dost Thou dispose of all things with Thine elect, to whom Thou offerest Thyself to be received in this Sacrament !

For this verily exceedeth all understanding ; this specially draweth the hearts of the devout, and inflameth their affections.

For even Thy true faithful ones, who dispose their whole life to amendment, from this most precious Sacrament oftentimes gain much grace of devotion, and love of virtue.

X. O the admirable and hidden grace of this Sacrament, which only the faithful ones of Christ do know ! but the unbelieving and such as are slaves unto sin, cannot have experience thereof.

In this Sacrament spiritual grace is conferred, and virtue which was lost is restored in the soul, and the beauty which by sin had been disfigured again returneth.

This grace is sometimes so great, that out of the fulness of devotion here given, not the mind only, but the weak body also, feeleth great increase of strength bestowed on it.

XI. Nevertheless our lukewarmness and negligence is exceedingly to be lamented and pitied, that we are not drawn with greater affection to receive Christ ; in whom doth consist all the hope of those that are to be saved, and all their merit.

For He Himself is our sanctification and redemption ; He Himself is the consolation of pilgrims, and the everlasting fruition of Saints.

It is therefore exceedingly to be lamented that many do so little consider this salutary Mystery, which causeth joy in Heaven, and preserveth the whole world.

Alas for the blindness and hardness of the human heart, that it does not more tenderly cherish so unspeakable a Gift ; but rather through the daily use thereof sinks into listless disregard of it !

XII. For if this most holy Sacrament were celebrated in one place only, and were consecrated by one only priest in the world ; with how great desires dost thou think would men be affected to that place, and towards such a priest of God, that they might be witnesses of the celebration of these divine Mysteries ?

But now many are made priests, and in many places Christ is offered ; that the grace and love of God to man may appear so much the greater, the more widely this sacred Communion is spread over the world.

Thanks be unto Thee, O merciful JESU, Thou eternal Shepherd, for that Thou hast vouchsafed to refresh us, who are poor and in a state of banishment, with Thy precious Body and Blood ; and to invite us to the receiving of these Mysteries by a message even from Thine own mouth, saying, 'Come unto Me all ye that labour and are heavy laden, and I will refresh you.'

CHAPTER II

THAT THE GREAT GOODNESS AND LOVE OF GOD IS EXHIBITED TO MAN IN THIS SACRAMENT

The Voice of the Disciple.

In confidence of Thy goodness and great mercy, O Lord, I draw near, as a sick person to the Healer, as one hungry and thirsty to the Fountain of Life, a needy wretch to the King of Heaven, a servant to his Lord, a creature to the Creator, a desolate soul to my own tender Comforter.

But whence is this to me, that Thou vouchsafest to come unto me?[1] what am I, that Thou shouldest grant Thine own self unto me?

How dare a sinner appear before Thee? and how is it that Thou dost vouchsafe to come unto a sinner?

Thou knowest Thy servant, and art well aware that he hath in him no good thing, for which Thou shouldest grant him this favour.

I confess therefore mine own vileness, I acknowledge Thy goodness, I praise Thy tender mercy, and give Thee thanks for this Thy transcendent love.

For Thou doest this for Thine own sake, not for any merits of mine; to the end that Thy goodness may be the better known unto me, Thy love more abundantly poured down, and Thy gracious humility the more eminently set forth.

Since therefore it is Thy pleasure, and Thou hast commanded that it should be so, this Thy condescension is also dearly pleasing unto me, and O that my iniquity may be no hindrance herein!

II. O most sweet and most benign Jesu, how great reverence and thanksgiving, together with perpetual praise, is due unto Thee for the receiving of Thy sacred

---

[1] Luke i. [43].

O

Body and Blood, whose preciousness no mortal man is able to express !

But on what shall my thoughts dwell at this Communion, in thus approaching unto my Lord, whom I am not able duly to honour, and yet whom I cannot but desire devoutly to receive?

What can I think on better and more profitable, than utterly to humble myself before Thee, and to exalt Thine infinite goodness above me ?

I praise Thee, my God, and will exalt Thee for ever : I do despise myself and cast myself down before Thee, into the deep of mine own vileness.

III. Behold, Thou art the Holy of holies, and I the scum of sinners !

Behold, Thou inclinest Thyself unto me, who am not worthy so much as to look up unto Thee !

Behold, Thou comest unto me ; it is Thy will to be with me, Thou invitest me to Thy banquet.

Thou art willing to give me heavenly food and bread of Angels to eat,[1] which is indeed no other than Thyself the Living Bread, which camest down from Heaven, and givest life unto the world.

IV. Behold, from whence doth this love proceed ! what a gracious condescension of Thine shineth forth herein ! how great thanks and praises are due unto Thee for these benefits !

O how salutary and profitable was Thy counsel, when Thou didst ordain It ! how sweet and pleasant the banquet, when Thou gavest Thyself to be our food !

O how admirable is this Thy working, O Lord, how mighty is Thy power, how unspeakable Thy truth !

For Thou didst speak the word and all things were made ;[2] and this was done which Thou Thyself commandest.

V. A matter of great admiration, worthy of all faith,

---

[1] Ps. lxxviii. [25] ; John vi. [33].
[2] Gen. i. ; Ps. cxlviii. [5].

and surpassing man's understanding, that Thou my Lord God, True God and man, shouldest offer Thyself wholly to us in a little Bread and Wine, and therein become our inexhaustible support.

Thou who art the Lord of the universe, and standest in need of none,[1] art pleased to dwell in us by means of this Thy Sacrament.

Do Thou preserve my heart and body undefiled, that with a cheerful and pure conscience I may be able very frequently * to celebrate, and * to receive to my ever-lasting health, those Mysteries, which Thou didst specially ordain and institute for Thine own honour, and for a never-ceasing memorial of Thyself.

VI. Rejoice, O my soul, and give thanks unto God, for so noble a gift, and so precious a consolation, left unto thee in this vale of tears.

For as often as thou callest to mind this Mystery, and receivest the Body of Christ, so often dost thou go over the work of thy redemption, and art made partaker of all the merits of Christ.

For the love of Christ is never diminished, and the greatness of His propitiation is never exhausted.

Therefore thou oughtest to dispose thyself hereunto by a constant fresh renewing of thy mind, and to weigh with attentive consideration the great Mystery of salvation.

So great, so new, and so joyful ought it to seem unto thee, when thou * celebratest or * partakest in these holy Mysteries, as if on this same day Christ first descending into the womb of the Virgin were become man, or hanging on the Cross did suffer and die for the salvation of mankind.

[2] Psalm xvi. [2].

* The parts between asterisks not to be used save by a Priest.

CHAPTER III

THAT IT IS PROFITABLE TO COMMUNICATE OFTEN

The Voice of the Disciple.

BEHOLD, O Lord, I come unto Thee, that it may be well with me through Thy gift, and that I may rejoice in Thy holy feast, which Thou, O God, hast in Thy goodness prepared for the poor.[1]

Behold in Thee is all whatsoever I can or ought to desire; Thou art my Salvation and my Redemption, my Hope and my Strength, my Honour and Glory.

Rejoice therefore this day the soul of Thy servant;[2] for unto Thee, O Lord JESU, have I lifted up my soul.

I do long to receive Thee now with devotion and reverence; I desire to bring Thee into my house, that with Zaccheus I may be counted worthy to be blessed by Thee, and to be numbered amongst the sons of Abraham.

My soul thirsteth to receive Thy Body and Blood; my heart longeth to be united with Thee.

II. Give Thyself to me, and it sufficeth; for besides Thee no comfort is available.

Without Thee I cannot be, and without Thy visitation I have no power to live.

And therefore I must needs often draw near unto Thee, and receive Thee for the medicine of my salvation; lest haply I faint in the way, if I be deprived of the heavenly Food.

For so, most merciful JESUS, Thou once didst say, preaching to the people, and curing divers diseases, 'I will not send them home fasting, lest they faint in the way.'[3]

Deal Thou therefore in like manner now with me,

---

[1] Psalm lxviii. [10].   [2] Psalm lxxxvi. [4].
[3] Matt. xv. [32]; Mark viii. [8].

who hast vouchsafed to leave Thyself in the Sacrament for the comfort of the faithful.

For Thou art the sweet refection of the soul ; and he that eateth Thee worthily, shall be partaker and heir of everlasting glory.

It is indeed necessary for me, who so often fall into error and sin, so quickly wax dull and faint, that by frequent prayer and confession, and receiving of Thy Holy Body and Blood, I renew, cleanse and inflame myself, lest haply, by too long abstaining, I fall away from my holy purposes.

III. For the imaginations of man are prone unto evil from his youth ;[1] and unless some divine remedy help him, he by-and-by falleth away to worse things.

This Holy Communion therefore draweth us back from evil and strengtheneth us in good.

For if I be now so often negligent and lukewarm when I communicate * or celebrate * ; what would become of me if I received not this remedy, and sought not after so great a help ?

* And although I may not be fit, nor well prepared to celebrate every day ; I will endeavour notwithstanding at due times to receive the divine Mysteries, and to be partaker of so great a Grace. *

For this is the one chief consolation of faithful souls, so long as they are absent from Thee in this mortal body; that being mindful of their God, they often receive their Beloved, with devout mind.

IV. O the wonderful condescension of Thy tender mercy towards us, that Thou O Lord God, the Creator and Giver of life to all Spirits, dost vouchsafe to come unto a poor soul, and with Thy whole Deity and Humanity abundantly to satisfy its famishing hunger !

O happy minds and blessed souls, who have the privilege of receiving Thee, their Lord God, with devout affection, and in so receiving Thee are permitted to be full of spiritual joy !

[1] Gen. viii. [21].

O how great a Lord do they entertain ! how beloved a Guest do they harbour ! how delightful a Companion do they receive ! how faithful a Friend do they welcome ! how lovely and noble a Spouse do they embrace ! even Him who is to be loved before all that are beloved, and above all things that can be desired.

O Thou my most sweet, most beloved ! let heaven and earth and all their ornaments be silent in Thy presence ; for what praise and beauty soever they have, it is received from Thy bounteous condescension, and shall never equal the grace and beauty of Thy Name, whose wisdom is beyond all numbers.[1]

CHAPTER IV

THAT MANY BENEFITS ARE BESTOWED UPON THEM THAT COMMUNICATE DEVOUTLY

The Voice of the Disciple.

O LORD my God, do Thou prevent Thy servant with the blessings of Thy sweetness,[2] that I may be enabled to approach worthily and devoutly to Thy glorious Sacrament.

Stir up my heart toward Thee, and set me free from heavy listlessness : visit me with Thy salvation,[3] that I may taste in spirit Thy sweetness, which plentifully lieth hid in this Sacrament as in a fountain.

Enlighten also mine eyes to behold so great a Mystery, and strengthen me with undoubting faith to believe it.

For it is Thy work, and no human power ; Thy sacred institution, not man's invention.

For of himself no man is able to comprehend and

[1] Psalm cxlvii. [5].   [2] Psalm xxi. [3].
[3] Psalm cvi. [4].

understand these things, which transcend even the exquisite skill of Angels.

What portion then of so high and sacred a Mystery shall I, unworthy sinner, dust and ashes, be able to search out and comprehend ?

II. O Lord, in the simplicity of my heart, with a good and firm faith, and at Thy commandment, I draw near unto Thee with hope and reverence ; and I do truly believe that Thou art here present in this Sacrament, both God and Man.

Thy will therefore is, that I should receive Thee, and that I should unite myself unto Thee in charity.

Whereupon I implore Thy mercy, and do crave Thy special Grace, to this end ; that I may wholly be dissolved and overflow with love towards Thee, and never hereafter suffer any consolation to enter in, which comes not from Thee.

For this most high and precious Sacrament is the health both of soul and body, the medicine for all spiritual languor ; hereby my vices are cured, my passions bridled, my temptations overcome or at least weakened ; greater grace is infused, virtue begun is increased, faith is confirmed, hope strengthened, and love inflamed and enlarged.

III. For Thou hast bestowed, and still oftentimes dost bestow many benefits in this Sacrament upon Thy beloved ones that communicate devoutly, O my God, the Protector of my soul, the Restorer of human weakness, and the Giver of all inward consolation.

For Thou impartest unto them much comfort against every variety of tribulation, and liftest them up from the depth of their own dejected state, to hope in Thy protection, and dost inwardly recreate and enlighten them with new Grace ; so that they who at first and before Communion felt themselves full of anxiety and heartlessness, afterwards, being refreshed with heavenly Meat and Drink, do find in themselves a change for the better.

And in such a way of dispensation as this dealest Thou with Thine elect, in order that they may truly acknowledge, and clearly prove, how great their own infirmity is, and what goodness and grace they obtain from Thee.

For they of themselves are cold, hard, and undevout; but by Thee they are enabled to become fervent, cheerful, and devout.

For who is there, that approaching humbly unto the fountain of sweetness, doth not carry away from thence at least some little sweetness?

Or who standing near a large fire, receiveth not some small heat therefrom?

And Thou art a fountain always full and overflowing; a fire ever burning and never going out.[1]

IV. Wherefore if I am not permitted to draw out of the full fountain itself, nor to drink my fill, I will notwithstanding set my lips to the mouth of this Heavenly conduit, that I may receive from thence at least some small drop to refresh my thirst, and may not quite wither away.

And though I cannot as yet be altogether Heavenly, nor so inflamed as the Cherubim and Seraphim, yet notwithstanding I will endeavour to apply myself earnestly to devotion, and to prepare my heart to obtain if it be but some small flame of divine fire, by the humble receiving of this life-giving Sacrament.

But whatsoever is hereunto wanting in me, O Merciful JESU, most Holy Saviour, do Thou in my behalf bountifully and graciously supply, Thou who hast vouchsafed to call us all unto Thee, saying, 'Come unto Me all ye that labour and are heavy laden, and I will refresh you.'[2]

V. I indeed labour in the sweat of my brows.[3] I am racked with grief of heart, I am burdened with sins, I am troubled with temptations, I am entangled and oppressed with many evil passions; and there is none to help me, none to deliver and save me, but Thou O Lord God my Saviour, to whom I commit myself and

---

[1] Isaiah xii. [3] ; Lev. vi. [13].   [2] Matt. xi. [28].
[3] Gen. iii. [19].

all that is mine, that Thou mayest keep watch over me, and bring me safe to life everlasting.

Receive me for the honour and glory of Thy Name, Thou who hast prepared Thy Body and Blood to be my meat and drink.

Grant, O Lord God, my Saviour, that by frequenting Thy Mysteries, the zeal of my devotion may grow and increase.

CHAPTER V

OF THE DIGNITY OF THIS SACRAMENT, AND OF THE MINISTERIAL FUNCTION

The Voice of the Beloved.

IF thou hadst the purity of Angels,[1] and the sanctity of Saint John Baptist, thou wouldst not be worthy either to receive this Sacrament thyself, or to administer It to others.

For it is not within the compass of the deserts of men, that man should consecrate and administer the Sacrament of Christ, and receive for food the bread of Angels.[3]

Grand is this Mystery; great too is the dignity of the Priests, to whom hath been granted that which is not permitted to Angels.

For none but Priests duly ordained in the Church, have power to celebrate this Sacrament, and to consecrate the Body of Christ.

The Priest is indeed the minister of God, using the word of God, by God's command and appointment: nevertheless God is there the principal Author, and invisible Worker; to whom all that He willeth is subject, and all that He commandeth is obedient.[3]

[1] Matt. xviii. [10].   [2] Psalm lxxviii. [25].
[3] Gen. i.; Ps. xlix. [7]; Rom. ix. [20].

II. * Thou oughtest then to trust God Almighty in this most excellent Sacrament, more than thine own sense, or any visible sign.

And therefore thou must approach to this holy work with fear and reverence.

Take diligent heed unto thyself,[1] and see what That is, whereof the ministry is delivered unto thee by the laying on of the Bishop's hand.

Behold, thou hast been made a priest, and consecrated to celebrate the Lord's Sacraments; see now that thou offer [the Christian] Sacrifice to God faithfully and devoutly, and at fit opportunities, and conduct thyself so, as that thou mayest be without reproof.

Thou hast not lightened thy burden, but art now bound with a straiter band of discipline, and art obliged to a more perfect degree of sanctity.

A Priest ought to be adorned with all graces, and to give example of good life to others.

His life and conversation[2] should not be in the popular and common ways of mankind, but with the Angels in Heaven, or with perfect men on earth.

III. A Priest clad in sacred garments is Christ's Deputy, that with all supplication and humility he may beseech God for himself and for the whole people.[3]

He hath both before and behind him the sign of the Lord's Cross, that he may continually be reminded of the Passion of Christ. He weareth the Cross on the Chasuble before him, that he may diligently look on Christ's footsteps, and earnestly study to follow them. Behind also, he is signed with the Cross, that he may cheerfully endure, for God's sake, any evils inflicted on him by others. He beareth the Cross before him, that he may mourn for his own sins,—and behind him, that he may with sympathy and tears lament for the faults of others also, and know that he hath been placed in the midst between God and the sinner.

Neither ought he to cease from prayer and holy oblation, till he prevail to obtain grace and mercy.

When a Priest doth celebrate [the Holy Eucharist],

[1] 1 Tim. iv. [16].   [2] Phil. iii. [20].   [3] Heb. v. [3].

he honoureth God, he rejoiceth the Angels, he edifieth the Church, he helpeth the living, [he commemorateth the departed,] and maketh himself partaker of all good things.

CHAPTER VI

AN ENQUIRY CONCERNING SPIRITUAL EXERCISE BEFORE COMMUNION

The Voice of the Disciple.

WHEN I weigh Thy worthiness, O Lord, and mine own vileness, I exceedingly tremble, and am confounded within myself.

For if I come not unto Thee, I fly from life ; and if I unworthily intrude myself, I incur Thy displeasure.

What therefore shall I do, O my God, my Helper and my Counsellor in all necessity ?

II. Teach Thou me the right way : appoint me some brief exercise, suitable to this Holy Communion.

For it is good for me to know how with devotion and reverence I should prepare my heart for Thee, for the receiving of Thy Sacrament to my soul's health, * or it may be also for the celebrating of so great and divine a Sacrifice. *

CHAPTER VII

OF THOROUGHLY SEARCHING OUR OWN CONSCIENCE, AND OF HOLY PURPOSES OF AMENDMENT

The Voice of the Beloved.

*ABOVE all things, with exceeding humility of heart, and with suppliant reverence, with a full faith, and dutiful anxiety for God's honour, ought God's Priest to come to celebrate, and to receive this Sacrament.

Examine diligently thy conscience, and to the utmost of thy power purify and make it clear, with true contrition and humble confession ; so as there may be nothing in thee, that may weigh heavy upon thee, or that may breed in thee remorse of conscience, and hinder thy free access to the throne of Grace.

Think with displeasure of all thy sins in general, and more particularly bewail and lament thy daily transgressions.

And if thou hast time, confess unto God in the secret of thine heart all the wretchedness of thy disordered passions.

II. Lament with pain and sighing that thou art yet so carnal and worldly, so unmortified in thy passions, so full of the motions of concupiscence.

So unwatchful over thy outward senses, so often entangled with many vain fancies :

So much inclined to outward things, so negligent in things inward and spiritual :

So prone to laughter and unbridled mirth, so hard and indisposed to tears and compunction :

So prompt to ease and pleasures of the flesh, so dull to zeal and strictness of life :

So curious to hear what is new, and to see what is beautiful ; so slack to embrace what is humble and mean :

So covetous of abundance, so niggardly in giving, so close in keeping :

So inconsiderate in speech, so reluctant to keep silence :

So unhandsome in manners, so fretful in conduct :

So eager about food, so deaf to the Word of God :

In such a hurry to rest, so slow to labour :

So wakeful after gossiping tales, so drowsy at the sacred Services :

So hasty to arrive at the end thereof, so inclined to be wandering and inattentive :

So negligent in the prayers, so lukewarm in celebrating, so dry and heartless in receiving the Holy Eucharist.

So quickly distracted, so seldom thoroughly self-collected :

So suddenly moved to anger, so apt to take displeasure against another :

So ready to judge, so severe to reprove :

So joyful at prosperity, so weak in adversity :

So often making many good resolutions, and yet bringing them at last to so poor effect.

III. These and other thy defects being confessed and bewailed with sorrow and great displeasure at thine own infirmity, make thou a firm resolution to be always amending thy life, and making progress in all that is good.

Then with full resignation and with thy entire will, offer up thyself to the honour of My Name, on the altar of thy heart a perpetual whole burnt offering, even thy body and soul, faithfully committing them unto Me.

And thus mayest thou be accounted worthy to draw near to celebrate this Eucharistical Sacrifice unto God, and to receive the Sacrament of My Body and Blood to thy soul's health. *

IV. For man hath no oblation more worthy, nor any greater for the destroying of sin, than to offer himself unto God purely and wholly, in and with the Holy Communion of Christ's Body and Blood.

And when a man shall have done what lieth in him, and shall be truly penitent, how often soever he shall come to Me for pardon and grace, 'as I live,' saith the Lord, 'who will not the death of a sinner, but rather that he be converted and live,¹ I will not remember his sins any more, but they shall all be forgiven him.'

¹ Ezek. xviii. [22, 23].

CHAPTER VIII

OF THE OBLATION OF CHRIST ON THE CROSS AND OF RESIGNATION OF OURSELVES

The Voice of the Beloved.

As I of Mine own will did offer up Myself unto God the Father for thy sins,[1] My hands stretched out on the cross, and My body stripped and laid bare, so that nothing remained in Me that was not wholly turned into a sacrifice for the appeasing of the divine Majesty:

In like manner oughtest thou also to offer thyself willingly unto Me every day in the Holy Communion, as a pure and sacred oblation, with all thy strength and affections, and to the utmost reach of thy inward faculties.

What do I require of thee more, than that thou study to resign thyself entirely unto Me?

Whatsoever thou givest besides thyself, is of no value in My sight, for I seek not thy gifts, but thee.[2]

II. As it would not suffice thee to have all things whatsoever, besides Me; so neither can it please Me, whatsoever thou givest, if thou offer not thyself.

Offer up thyself unto Me, and give thyself wholly for God, and thy offering shall be acceptable.

Behold, I offered up Myself wholly unto My Father for thee; I give also My whole Body and Blood for thy food, that I might be wholly thine, and that thou mightest continue Mine to the end.

But if thou stand upon thyself, and dost not offer thyself up freely unto My will, the oblation is not complete, neither will there be entire union between us.

Therefore a free offering up of thyself into the hands of God ought to go before all thine actions, if thou desire to obtain liberty and grace.

[1] Isaiah liii. [5]; Heb. ix. [28].   [2] Prov. xxiii. [26].

For this is the cause why so few become illuminated and inwardly free, because they cannot endure wholly to deny themselves.

My sentence standeth sure, 'Unless a man forsake all, he cannot be My disciple.'[1] If thou therefore desire to be My disciple, offer up thyself unto Me with thy whole affections.

CHAPTER IX

THAT WE OUGHT TO OFFER UP OURSELVES AND ALL THAT IS OURS UNTO GOD, AND TO PRAY FOR ALL

· *The Voice of the Disciple.*

THINE, O Lord, are all things that are in heaven, and that are in earth.[2] ·

I desire to offer up myself unto Thee, as a free oblation, and to continue Thine for ever.

O Lord, in the simplicity of my heart I offer myself unto Thee this day to be Thy servant for ever, in humble submission, and for a sacrifice of perpetual praise.

Receive Thou me, with this holy Oblation of Thy precious Body; which Offering I make to Thee this day in the presence of Angels invisibly attending; and may this further the salvation of myself and of all Thy people.

II. Lord, I offer unto Thee, on Thy propitiatory altar, all my sins and offences, which I have committed before Thee and Thy holy Angels, from the day wherein I first could sin even to this hour; that Thou mayest consume and burn them, one and all, with the fire of Thy love, and do away all the stains of my sins, and cleanse my conscience from all offences, and restore to me Thy grace which I lost by sin, fully

[1] Luke xiv. [33].   [2] Psalm xxiv. [1].

forgiving me all, and admitting me mercifully to the kiss of peace.

III. What can I do in regard of my sins, but humbly confess and bewail them,[1] and unceasingly entreat Thy propitiation?

I entreat Thee, hear me propitiously, when I stand before Thee my God.

All my sins are exceedingly displeasing to me; I will never more commit them; but for them I do grieve, and will grieve as long as I live, being resolved to practise penitence, and to the utmost of my power to make restitution.

Forgive me, O God, forgive me my sins for the sake of Thy holy Name; save Thou my soul, which Thou hast redeemed with Thy precious Blood.

Behold I commit myself unto Thy mercy, I resign myself into Thy hands.

Deal with me according to Thy goodness, not according to my wickedness and iniquity.

IV. I offer up also unto Thee all that is good in me, though it be very small and imperfect, in order that Thou mayest amend and sanctify it, that Thou mayest make it grateful and acceptable unto Thee, and always be perfecting it more and more; and bring me also, slothful and unprofitable poor creature as I am, to a good and blessed end.

V. Moreover I offer up unto Thee all the pious desires of devout persons, the necessities of parents, friends, brethren, sisters, and of all those who are dear unto me, or who have done good either to myself or others for Thy love.

Also I commend unto Thee, all that have desired and begged of me to pray for them and all theirs. . . . .

That all may feel the present help of Thy grace, the aid of Thy consolation, protection from dangers, deliverance from pain; and that being rescued from all evils, they may with joy return abundant thanksgivings unto Thee.

[1] Psalm xxxii. [5].

VI. I offer up also unto Thee my Sacramental prayers and intercessions, for those especially who have in any matter hurt, grieved, or found fault with me, or who have done me any damage or displeasure.

For all those also, whom at any time I may have vexed, troubled, burdened, and scandalized, by words or deeds, knowingly or in ignorance ; that Thou wouldst grant us all equally pardon for our sins, and for our offences against each other.

Take away from our hearts, O Lord, all suspiciousness, indignation, wrath, and contention, and whatsoever may hurt charity, and lessen brotherly love.

Have mercy, O Lord, have mercy on those that crave Thy mercy, give Grace unto them that stand in need thereof, and make us such as that we may be worthy to enjoy Thy Grace, and go forward to life eternal. Amen.

CHAPTER X

THAT THE HOLY COMMUNION IS NOT LIGHTLY TO BE FORBORNE

The Voice of the Beloved.

THOU oughtest often to have recourse to the Fountain of grace and of divine mercy, to the Fountain of goodness and of all purity ; that thou mayest be healed of thy sins and passions, and obtain to be made more strong and vigilant against all the temptations and deceits of the devil.

The Enemy knowing what exceeding great profit and restorative aid comes by the Holy Communion, endeavoureth by all means and occasions to withdraw and hinder faithful and devout persons from partaking therein.

II. Thus it is that some persons, when they are

P

preparing to fit themselves for Holy Communion, suffer from the insinuations of Satan worse than before.

That wicked spirit himself (as it is written in Job) cometh amongst the sons of God,[1] to trouble them according to his accustomed malice, or to render them over-fearful and perplexed, that so he may diminish their affections, or by direct assaults take away their faith ; to the end he may prevail on them if possible either altogether to forbear communicating, or at least to come with lukewarmness.

But there is no heed at all to be taken of these his crafty and fanciful suggestions, be they never so filthy and hideous, but all such vain imaginations are to be turned back upon his own head.

They must despise and laugh to scorn the miserable wretch, nor dare to omit the Holy Communion on account of his assaults, or for the troubles which he raiseth within them.

III. Oftentimes also an over-great solicitude for the obtaining a certain degree of devotion, and some anxiety or other about the confession of sins, perplexeth and hindereth them.

Follow thou herein the counsel of the wise,[2] and lay aside anxiety and scrupulousness ; for it hinders the Grace of God, and overthrows the devotion of the mind.

Do not omit the Holy Communion for every small vexation and trouble, but rather proceed at once to confess thy sins, and cheerfully forgive others whatever offences they have done against thee.[3]

And if thou hast offended any, humbly crave pardon, and God will readily forgive thee.

IV. What availeth it to delay long the confession of thy sins, or to defer the Holy Communion ?

Make thyself thoroughly clean as soon as possible, spit out the poison with all speed, make haste to apply this sovereign Remedy, and thou shalt find it to be better with thee, than if thou long defer it.

---

[1] Job i. [6].   [2] Prov. xiii. [1].   [3] Matt. v. [24].

If thou omit it to-day for one cause, perhaps to-morrow another of greater force may occur to thee; and so thou mayest be hindered a long time from Communion, and grow more and more unfit.

As quickly as ever thou canst, shake off from thyself thy present heaviness and sloth, for it is of no use to continue long in disquietness, or to be going on long with a disturbed [conscience], and for every-day impediments to sequester thyself from Divine service.

Yea, it is most exceedingly hurtful to defer the Communion long, for it usually brings on a heavy spiritual drowsiness.

Alas, some persons, lukewarm and undisciplined, do willingly delay confession, and defer the Holy Communion, lest they should be obliged to keep a stricter watch over themselves.

V. O how poor and mean is their love, how weak their devotion, who so easily put off the Holy Communion!

How happy is he and how acceptable to God, who so ordereth his life, and in such purity guardeth his conscience, that he is prepared and well-disposed to communicate even every day, if it were in his power, and might be done without others taking notice.

If a person do sometimes abstain out of humility, or by reason of some lawful cause preventing him, he is to be commended so far as it arises from a feeling of reverence.

But if a spiritual drowsiness have crept over him, he must stir himself up, and do what lieth in him, and the Lord will assist his desire, for the good will he hath thereto, which is what God doth chiefly respect.

VI. But when any lawful hindrance doth happen, he will yet always have a good will, and a pious intention to communicate, and so shall he not lose the fruit of the Sacrament.

For it is in the power of any devout person every day and every hour profitably and without let to draw near to Christ in spiritual Communion.

And yet on certain days, and at time appointed,

he ought to receive Sacramentally, with affectionate reverence, the Body and Blood of his Redeemer, and rather seek the honour and glory of God, than his own comfort.[1]

For he communicateth mystically, and is invisibly refreshed, as often as he devoutly calleth to mind the mystery of the Incarnation and the Passion of Christ, and is inflamed with the love of Him.

VII. He that prepareth not himself, except only when a festival draweth near, or when custom compelleth him thereunto, shall too often be unprepared.

Blessed is he that offereth up himself as a whole burnt offering to the Lord, as often as he doth either administer or receive the Holy Communion.

* Be not too slow nor yet hurried in celebrating, but keep the good accustomed manner of those with whom thou livest.

Thou oughtest not to be tedious, and so troublesome to others, but to observe the received custom, according to the appointment of our fathers ; and rather to yield thyself up to the edification of others, than to thine own devotion or feelings. *

CHAPTER XI

THAT THE BODY AND BLOOD OF CHRIST AND THE HOLY SCRIPTURES ARE MOST NECESSARY UNTO A FAITHFUL SOUL

The Voice of the Disciple.

O BLESSED Lord JESUS, how great is the blessedness of the devout soul that feasteth with Thee in Thy banquet : where there is set no other food to be eaten but Thyself, the only Beloved, and most to be desired above all the desires of the heart !

---

[1] 1 Cor. xi. [23—26].

To me also it would be indeed a blessed thing, in Thy presence to pour forth tears from the very bottom of my heart, and with the grateful Magdalene to wash Thy feet with tears.[1]

But where now is that devotion ? where that plentiful effusion of holy tears ?

Surely in the sight of Thee and Thy holy Angels, my whole heart ought to be inflamed, and even to weep for joy.

For in this Sacrament I have Thee truly present, though hidden under another representation.

II. For to look upon Thee in Thine own Divine brightness, mine eyes would not be able to endure ; nor could even the whole world stand in the splendour of the glory of Thy Majesty.

Herein then Thou hast regard to my weakness, that Thou dost veil thyself under this Sacramental sign.

Him do I really possess and adore, whom the Angels adore in Heaven : I however, for the present and for a while, by faith ; but they by sight, and without a veil.

As to me, I ought to be content with the light of true faith, and therein to walk, till the day of everlasting brightness shall dawn, and the shadows of figures pass away.

But when that which is perfect is come, the use of Sacraments shall cease ; [2] because the Blessed, in their Heavenly Glory, need not any Sacramental remedy :

For they rejoice without end in the presence of God, beholding His glory face to face ; and being transformed from brightness to brightness, even that of the incomprehensible Deity, they taste the WORD of God made flesh, as He was from the beginning, and as He abideth for ever.

III. Whilst I think on these wonderful things, it becometh heavy and wearisome unto me, even all spiritual comfort whatever ; because as long as I behold

[1] Luke vii. [38].   [2] 1 Cor. xiii. [10].

not my Lord openly in His own glory, I account as nothing all that I see or hear in this world.

Thou art my witness, O God, that nothing can comfort me, no creature can give me rest, but only Thou my God, whom I earnestly desire to contemplate everlastingly.

But this is not possible, so long as I linger in this mortality.

Therefore I must frame myself to much patience; and submit myself to Thee in every desire.

For even Thy Saints, O Lord, who now rejoice with Thee in the kingdom of Heaven, whilst they lived, waited in faith and in great patience for the coming of Thy glory.[1]

What they believed, I believe; what they hoped, I hope; whither they are arrived by Thy grace, I trust I shall come.

In the meantime I will walk in faith, strengthened by the examples of the Saints.

I have also holy books for my comfort and for the glass of my life; and above all these, I have Thy most Holy Body and Blood for a singular remedy and refuge.

IV. For I perceive two things to be very particularly necessary for me in this life, without which this miserable life would be insupportable unto me.

Whilst I am detained in the prison of this body, I acknowledge myself to stand in need of two things, namely, food and light.

Unto me then thus weak and helpless Thou hast given Thy sacred Body, for the refreshment both of my soul and body;[2] and Thy word Thou hast set as a lamp unto my feet.[3]

Without these two I should not well be able to live; for the word of God is the light of my soul, and Thy Sacrament the Bread of life.

These also may be called the two tables, set on the

---

[1] Heb. x. [35, 36]; xi. [39, 40].   [2] John vi. [51].
[3] Psalm cxix. [105].

one side and on the other, in the treasury and jewel-house of the Holy Church.[1]

One table is that of the Sacred Altar, having the holy bread, that is, the precious Body of Christ; the other is that of the Divine Law, containing holy doctrine, teaching men the right faith, and stedfastly leading them onward even to that within the veil, where is the Holy of Holies.

Thanks be unto Thee, O Lord Jesu, Thou Light of everlasting Light, for that table of sacred doctrine, which Thou hast prepared for us by Thy servants the Prophets and Apostles and other teachers.

V. Thanks be unto Thee, O Thou Creator and Redeemer of mankind, who to manifest Thy love to the whole world, hast prepared a great supper,[2] wherein Thou hast set before us to be eaten, not the typical lamb, but Thine own most sacred Body and Blood;[3] rejoicing all the faithful with this sacred banquet, and replenishing them to the full with the Cup of Salvation,[4] in which are all the delights of Paradise; and the holy Angels do feast with us, but yet with a more happy sweetness.

VI. O how great and honourable is the office of God's Priests! to whom it is given with sacred words to consecrate [the Sacrament of] the LORD of Glory; with their lips to bless, with their hands to hold, with their own mouth to receive, and also to administer to others.

O how clean ought those hands to be, how pure that mouth, how holy that body, how unspotted that heart, where the Author of purity so often entereth!

Nothing but what is holy, no word but what is good and profitable, ought to proceed from the mouth of the Priest, of him who so often receiveth the Sacrament of Christ.

VII. Simple and chaste ought to be the eyes that are

---

[1] Psalm xxiii. [5]'; Heb. ix. [2—4], xiii. [10].
[2] Luke xiv. [16].   [3] John vi. [53—56].
[4] Psalm xxiii. [5]; Wisd. xvi. [20, 21].

wont to behold the Body of Christ; the hands should be pure and lifted up to Heaven, that use to touch the Creator of Heaven and earth.

Unto the Priest more especially it is said in the Law, 'Be ye holy, for that I the LORD your God am holy.'[1]

VIII. *O Almighty God, do Thou assist us with Thy grace, that we who have undertaken the office of the Priesthood, may be able to wait on Thee worthily and devoutly, in all purity, and with a good conscience.

And if we live not in so great innocency as we ought to do, grant to us at the least worthily to lament the sins which we have committed; and in the spirit of humility, and with the full purpose of a good will, to serve Thee more earnestly for the time to come.*

CHAPTER XII

THAT HE WHO IS ABOUT TO COMMUNICATE WITH CHRIST OUGHT TO PREPARE HIMSELF WITH GREAT DILIGENCE

The Voice of the Beloved.

I AM the Lover of purity and the Giver of all sanctity.

I seek a pure heart, and there is the place of my rest.[2]

'Make ready for Me a large upper room furnished,[3] and I will keep the passover at thy house with My Disciples.'

If thou wilt have Me come unto thee, and remain with thee; purge out the old leaven,[4] and make clean the habitation of thy heart.

[1] Levit. xix. [2], xx. [26].
[2] Ps. xxiv. [4]; Matt. v. [8].
[3] Mark xiv. [14, 15]; Luke xxii. [11, 12].
[4] 1 Cor. v. [7].

Shut out the whole world,[1] and all the throng of sins: sit thou as it were a sparrow alone upon the house-top, and think over thy transgressions in the bitterness of thy soul.

For every one that loveth will prepare the best and fairest place for his beloved ; for herein is known the affection of him that entertaineth his beloved.

II. Know thou notwithstanding, that no merit of any action of thine is able to make this preparation sufficient, although thou shouldest prepare thyself a whole year together, and have nothing else in thy mind.

But it is out of My mere grace and favour that thou art permitted to approach My table ; as if a beggar were invited to a rich man's dinner, and he hath no other return to make to him for his benefits, but to humble himself and give him thanks.

Do what lieth in thee, and do it diligently ; not for custom, not for necessity, but with fear and reverence and affection, receive the Body and Blood of thy beloved Lord God, when He vouchsafeth to come unto thee.

I am He that have called thee, I have commanded it to be done, I will supply what is wanting in thee ; come thou and receive Me.

III. When I bestow on thee the grace of Devotion, give thanks to thy God ; [for it is given thee] not because thou art worthy, but because I have had mercy on thee.

If thou have it not, but rather dost feel thyself dry, be instant in prayer, sigh and knock, and give not over until thou art meet to receive some crumb or drop of saving Grace.

Thou hast need of Me, I have no need of thee.

Neither comest thou to sanctify Me, but I come to sanctify thee, and make thee better.

Thou comest that thou mayest be sanctified by Me, and united unto Me ; that thou mayest receive new

---

[1] Exod. xxiv. [18].

grace, and be stirred up anew to amendment of life.

See thou neglect not this Grace, but prepare thy heart with all diligence, and receive thy Beloved into thy soul.

IV. Thou oughtest however not only to prepare thyself to devotion before Communion, but carefully also to preserve thyself therein, after thou hast received the Sacrament.

Nor is the careful guard of thyself afterwards less required, than devout preparation before.

For a good guard afterwards is the best preparation again for the obtaining of greater grace.

For if a person gives himself up at once too much to outward consolations, he is rendered thereby exceedingly indisposed to devotion.

Beware of much talk,[1] remain in some secret place, and enjoy thy God: for thou hast Him, whom all the world cannot take from thee.

I am He, to whom thou oughtest wholly to give up thyself, that so thou mayest now live no longer in thyself, but in me, free from all anguish of mind.

CHAPTER XIII

THAT THE DEVOUT SOUL OUGHT WITH THE WHOLE HEART TO SEEK UNION WITH CHRIST IN THE SACRAMENT

The Voice of the Disciple.

WOULD that I might obtain this favour, Lord, to find Thee alone and by Thyself, to open unto Thee my whole heart, and enjoy Thee even as my soul desireth; and that henceforth none may look upon me, nor any creature move me, nor have regard to me; but that

---

[1] Prov. x. [19].

Thou alone mayest speak unto me, and I to Thee, as the beloved is wont to speak to his beloved, and friend to feast with friend.[1]

This I beg, this I long for, that I may be wholly united unto Thee, and may withdraw my heart from all created things, and by means of sacred Communion, and the frequent celebrating thereof, may learn more and more to relish things heavenly and eternal.

Ah, Lord God, when shall I be wholly united to Thee, and absorbed by Thee, and become altogether forgetful of myself?

'Thou in me, and I in Thee;'[2] so also grant that we may both continue together in one.

II. Verily, Thou art my Beloved, the Choicest amongst thousands,[3] in whom my soul is well pleased to dwell all the days of her life.

Verily, Thou art my Peacemaker, in whom is highest peace and true rest, out of whom is labour and sorrow and infinite misery.

Verily, Thou art a God that hidest Thyself,[4] and Thy counsel is not with the wicked, but Thy speech is with the humble and simple of heart.[5]

O how sweet is Thy Spirit,[6] O Lord, who to the end Thou mightest shew forth Thy sweetness toward Thy children, dost vouchsafe to refresh them with the Bread which is full of all sweetness, even That which cometh down from Heaven.

Surely there is no other nation so great,[7] that hath gods so nigh unto them, as Thou our God art present to all Thy faithful ones, unto whom for their daily comfort, and for the raising up of their hearts to Heaven, Thou bestowest Thyself to be eaten and enjoyed.

III. For what other nation is there of such high renown, as the Christian people?

Or what creature under Heaven is there so beloved,

---

[1] Exod. xxxiii. [11]; Cant. viii. [1, 2].
[2] John xv. [4].   [3] Cant. v. [10].
[4] [Isa. xlv. 15.]   [5] Prov. iii. [34].
[6] Wisd. xii. [1].   [7] Deut. iv. [7].

as the devout soul, into which God Himself entereth, to nourish it with His glorious Flesh?

O unspeakable grace! O admirable condescension! O unmeasurable love specially bestowed on man!

But what return shall I make to the Lord for this grace,[1] for charity so unparalleled?

There is nothing else that I am able to present more acceptable, than to offer my heart wholly to my God, and to unite it most inwardly unto Him.

Then shall all my inward parts rejoice, when my soul shall be perfectly united unto God.

Then will He say unto me, 'If thou art willing to be with Me, I am willing to be with thee.'

And I will answer Him, 'Vouchsafe, O Lord, to remain with me, I will gladly be with Thee.

'This is my whole desire, that my heart be united unto Thee.'

CHAPTER XIV

OF THE FERVENT DESIRE OF SOME DEVOUT PERSONS TO RECEIVE THE BODY AND BLOOD OF CHRIST

The Voice of the Disciple.

O how great is the abundance of Thy sweetness, O Lord, which Thou hast laid up for them that fear Thee![2]

When I call to mind some devout persons, who approach to Thy Sacrament, O Lord, with the greatest devotion and affection, I am oftentimes confounded and blush within myself, that I am come with such lukewarmness, yea coldness, to Thy Altar and the Table of sacred Communion.

I grieve to think that I remain so dry, and without

---

[1] Psalm cxvi. [12].   [2] Psalm xxxi. [19].

affection of heart; that I am not wholly inflamed in Thy presence, O my God, nor so earnestly drawn and affected, as many devout persons have been, who out of a vehement desire of the Communion, and a feeling affection of heart, were unable to restrain themselves from weeping; but with the mouth of their hearts and bodies alike, they from their inmost vitals panted after Thee, O God, the Fountain of life, not being otherwise able to allay or satisfy their hunger, but only by receiving Thy Body with all delight and spiritual eagerness.

II. O the truly ardent faith of those persons! amounting to a probable evidence of Thy sacred Presence.

For they truly know their Lord in the breaking of bread,[1] whose heart within them so vehemently burneth, whilst Thou, O blessed JESU, dost walk and converse with them.

Such affectionateness and devotion as this, love and fervency so vehement, are too often far from me.

Be Thou favourable unto me, O JESU, merciful, sweet and gracious Lord, and grant to me Thy poor needy creature, sometimes at least in this Holy Communion to feel if it be but a small portion of Thy hearty affectionate love; that my Faith may become more strong, my Hope in Thy goodness may be increased, and that Charity once perfectly kindled within me, after the tasting of this Heavenly Manna, may never decay.

III. Thy mercy however is well able to grant me even the Grace which I long for, and, in the day when it shall please Thee, to visit me most benignantly with the Spirit of fervour.

For although I burn not with desire vehement as theirs who are so especially devoted unto Thee, yet notwithstanding, by Thy Grace, I have a desire for this great inflamed desire, praying and longing that I may participate with all such Thy fervent lovers, and be numbered among them in their holy company.

[1] Luke xxiv [32, 35].

CHAPTER XV

THAT THE GRACE OF DEVOTION IS OBTAINED BY HUMILITY AND DENIAL OF OURSELVES

The Voice of the Beloved.

Thou oughtest to seek the grace of Devotion earnestly, to ask it fervently, to wait for it with patience and confidence, to receive it with gratefulness, to keep it humbly, to work with it diligently, and to commit the term and manner of this heavenly visitation to God, until it shall please Him to come unto thee.

Thou oughtest especially to humble thyself, when thou feelest inwardly little or no devotion ; but yet not to be too much dejected, nor to grieve inordinately.

God often giveth in one short moment, that which He for a long time denied ; He giveth sometimes in the end, that which in the beginning of thy prayer He deferred to give.

II. If Grace should be always presently given, and should be at hand ever with a wish, weak man could not well bear it.

Therefore the grace of Devotion is to be waited for, with good hope and humble patience.

Nevertheless, do thou impute it to thyself, and to thine own sins, when this grace is not given thee, or when it is secretly taken away.

It is sometimes but a small matter that hindereth and hideth Grace from us ; at least if any thing can be called small, and not rather a weighty matter, which obstructeth so great a good.

And if thou remove this, be it great or small, and perfectly overcome it, thou wilt have thy desire.

III. For immediately, as soon as thou givest thyself to God from thy whole heart, and seekest neither this nor that, according to thine own pleasure or will, but settlest thyself wholly in Him, thou shalt find thyself united and at peace ; for nothing can afford so sweet a relish, nothing be so delightful, as the good pleasure of the Divine will.

Whosoever therefore, with a single heart lifts up his intention to God, and keeps himself clear of all inordinate liking or disliking of any created thing, he shall be the most fit to receive Grace, and meet for the gift of true Devotion.

For the Lord bestoweth His blessings there, where He findeth the vessels empty.

And the more perfectly a person forsaketh these low things, and the more he by contempt of himself dieth to himself, so much the more speedily Grace cometh, the more plentifully doth it enter in, and the higher doth it lift up the free heart.

IV. Then shall he see, and flow together, and wonder, and his heart shall be enlarged [1] within him, because the hand of the Lord is with him, and he hath put himself wholly into His hand, even for ever and ever.

Behold, thus shall the man be blessed, who seeketh God with his whole heart, and receiveth not his soul in vain.

This man in receiving the Holy Eucharist, obtaineth the great Grace of Divine Union ; because it is not to his own devotion and comfort that he hath regard, but above all devotion and comfort to the honour and glory of God.

---

[1] Isa. lx. [5].

CHAPTER XVI

THAT WE OUGHT TO LAY OPEN OUR NECESSITIES TO CHRIST AND TO CRAVE HIS GRACE

The Voice of the Disciple.

O THOU most sweet and loving Lord, whom I now desire to receive with all devotion, Thou knowest mine infirmities, and the necessities which I endure ; in how great evils and sins I am involved ; how often I am weighed down, tempted, disturbed, and defiled by them.

Unto Thee I come for remedy, I entreat of Thee consolation and support.

I speak to Thee, who knowest all things, to whom all my inward thoughts are open, and who alone canst perfectly comfort and help me.

Thou knowest what good things I stand in most need of, and how poor I am in all virtue.

II. Behold, I stand before Thee poor and naked, calling for grace, and imploring mercy.

Refresh Thy hungry supplicant, inflame my coldness with the fire of Thy love, enlighten my blindness with the brightness of Thy presence.

Do Thou for me turn all earthly things into bitterness, all things grievous and contrary into patience, all low and created things into contempt and oblivion.

Lift up my heart to Thee in Heaven, and send me not away to wander over the earth.

Be Thou alone sweet unto me, from henceforth for evermore ; for Thou alone art my meat and drink, my love and my joy, my sweetness and all my good.

III. O that with Thy Presence Thou wouldest wholly inflame, consume, and transform me into Thyself ; that I might be made one Spirit with Thee,[1] by the grace of inward Union, and by the meltings of ardent love !

[1] 1 Cor. vi. [17].

Suffer me not to go away from Thee hungry and dry, but deal mercifully with me, as oftentimes Thou hast dealt wonderfully with Thy saints.

What marvel is it if I should be wholly inflamed by Thee, and of myself decay and come to nothing ; since Thou art Fire always burning and never decaying, Love purifying the heart, and enlightening the understanding.

CHAPTER XVII

OF FERVENT LOVE AND VEHEMENT DESIRE TO RECEIVE CHRIST

The Voice of the Disciple.

WITH deep devotion and ardent love, with all affection and fervour of heart, I desire to receive Thee, O Lord, as many Saints and devout persons have desired Thee, when they were partakers of Thy Holy Communion ; who in holiness of life were to Thee most pleasing, and who in devotion also were most fervent.

O my God, everlasting Love, my whole Good, Happiness which can have no limit, I do desire to receive Thee with the most earnest affection, and the most suitable awe and reverence, that any of the Saints ever had, or could feel toward Thee.

II. And although I be unworthy to entertain all those feelings of devotion, nevertheless I offer unto Thee the whole affection of my heart, as if I were the only person who had all those most grateful, most ardent longings after Thee.

Yea, and all that a dutiful mind can conceive and desire, I do, with the deepest reverence and most inward affection, offer and present unto Thee.

Q

I desire to reserve nothing to myself, but freely and most cheerfully to sacrifice unto Thee myself and all that is mine.

O Lord my God, my Creator and my Redeemer, I do desire to receive Thee this day, with such affection, reverence, praise and honour, with such gratitude, worthiness and love with such faith, hope and purity, as Thy most holy Mother, the glorious Virgin Mary, received and desired Thee, when to the Angel who declared unto her glad tidings of the mystery of the Incarnation, she humbly and devoutly answered, ' Behold the handmaid of the Lord, be it unto me according to Thy word.' [1]

III. And as Thy blessed forerunner, the most excellent among the Saints, John Baptist, rejoicing in Thy presence, leaped for joy of the Holy Ghost, whilst he was yet shut up in his mother's womb ; [2] and afterwards seeing JESUS walking among men, humbled himself very greatly, and said with devout affection, ' The friend of the bridegroom that standeth and heareth him, rejoiceth greatly because of the bridegroom's voice ; ' [3] in like manner do I also wish to be inflamed with great and holy desires, and to offer myself up to Thee from my whole heart.

Wherefore also for myself, and for all such as are commended to me in prayer, I offer and present unto Thee the triumphant joys, the ardent affections, the mental ecstacies, the supernatural illuminations and celestial visions of all devout hearts, with all the virtues and praises celebrated and to be celebrated by all creatures in Heaven, and in earth ; that by all Thou mayest worthily be praised and glorified for ever.

IV. Receive, O Lord my God, my wishes and desires of giving Thee infinite praise, and blessing that hath no bounds, which according to the measure of Thine ineffable greatness, are most justly due unto Thee.

These praises I render unto Thee, and long to render

[1] Luke i. [38].   [2] Luke i. [44].
          [3] John iii. [29]

them every day and every moment. And with all entreaty and affectionateness I do invite and beseech all Heavenly spirits, and all Thy faithful servants, to render with me thanks and praises unto Thee.

V. Let all people, nations, and languages praise Thee,[1] and magnify Thy holy and most delicious Name with highest exultation and ardent devotion.

And let all who reverently and devoutly celebrate Thy most high Sacrament, and receive It with full faith, be accounted worthy to find grace and mercy at Thy hands, and pray with humble supplication in behalf of me a sinner.

And when they shall have attained to their desired devotion, and joyful Union with Thee, and shall have departed from Thy Holy Heavenly Table, well comforted and marvellously refreshed, may they vouchsafe to remember poor me.

CHAPTER XVIII

THAT A MAN SHOULD NOT BE A CURIOUS SEARCHER INTO THE HOLY SACRAMENT, BUT AN HUMBLE FOLLOWER OF CHRIST, SUBMITTING HIS SENSE TO DIVINE FAITH.

The Voice of the Beloved.

Thou oughtest to beware of curious and unprofitable searching into this most profound Sacrament, if thou wilt not be plunged into the depths of doubt.

'He that is a searcher of My Majesty, shall be overpowered by the glory of it:'[2] God is able to work more than man can understand.

A dutiful and humble enquiry after the Truth, is

[1] Psalm cxvii.   [2] Prov. xxv. [27. Lat. vers.]

allowable, provided we be always ready to be taught, and that we study to walk according to the sound opinions of the Fathers.

II. It is a blessed simplicity when a man leaves the difficult ways of questions and disputings, and goes on forward in the plain and firm path of God's commandments.

Many have lost devotion, whilst they sought to search into things too high.

Faith is required at thy hands, and a sincere life; not height of understanding, nor the depth of the mysteries of God.

If thou dost not understand, nor conceive the things that are beneath thee, how shalt thou comprehend those which are above thee?

Submit thyself unto God, and humble thy sense to faith, and the light of knowledge shall be given thee, in such degree as shall be profitable and necessary for thee.

III. Some are grievously tempted about faith and the Holy Sacrament; but this is not to be imputed to themselves, but rather to the enemy.

Be not thou anxious herein; do not dispute with thine own thoughts, nor give any answer to doubts suggested by the devil; but trust the words of God, trust His Saints and Prophets, and the wicked enemy will flee from thee.

It oftentimes is very profitable to the servant of God to endure such things.

For the devil tempteth not unbelievers and sinners, whom he hath already secure possession of; but faithful and religious devout persons he in various ways tempteth and disquieteth.

IV. Go forward therefore with simple and undoubting faith, and with the reverence of a supplicant draw thou near to the Holy Sacrament; and whatsoever thou art not able to understand, commit securely to Almighty God.

God deceiveth thee not; he is deceived that trusteth too much to himself.

God walketh with the simple,[1] revealeth Himself to the humble, giveth understanding to the little ones, openeth the sense to pure minds, and hideth Grace from the curious and proud.

Human reason is feeble and may be deceived, but true Faith cannot be deceived.

V. All reason and natural search ought to follow Faith, not to go before it, nor to break in upon it.

For Faith and Love do here specially take the lead, and work in hidden ways, in this most holy, most supremely excellent Sacrament.

God, who is eternal, and incomprehensible, and of infinite power, doeth things great and unsearchable in Heaven and in earth, and there is no tracing out of His marvellous works.

If the works of God were such, as that they might be easily comprehended by human reason, they could not be justly called marvellous or unspeakable.

[1] Psalm xix. [7], cxix. [130] ; Matt. xi. [25].

THE END

Printed in England at the Oxford University Press

The World's Classics

THE best recommendation of **The World's Classics** is the books themselves, which have earned unstinted praise from critics and all classes of the public. Some two million copies have been sold, and of the volumes already published nearly one-half have gone into a second, third, fourth, fifth, sixth, seventh, eighth, ninth, or tenth impression. It is only possible to give so much for the money when large sales are certain. The clearness of the type, the quality of the paper, the size of the page, the printing, and the binding—from the cheapest to the best—cannot fail to commend themselves to all who love good literature presented in worthy form. That a high standard is insisted upon is proved by the list of books already published and of those on the eve of publication. A great feature is the brief critical introductions written by leading authorities of the day. The volumes of The World's Classics are obtainable, bound in cloth and leather, as given on page 1; and special attention is directed to the sultan-red limp leather style for presentation.

The Pocket Edition is printed on **thin opaque paper**, by means of which the bulk is greatly reduced.

January, 1918

LIST OF THE SERIES

The figures in parentheses denote the number of the book in the series

List of the Series—*continued*

List of the Series—*continued*

List of the Series—*continued*

List of the Series—*continued*

List of the Series—*continued*

HUMPHREY MILFORD
OXFORD UNIVERSITY PRESS
LONDON, EDINBURGH, GLASGOW
NEW YORK, TORONTO, MELBOURNE, BOMBAY
CAPE TOWN, & SHANGHAI

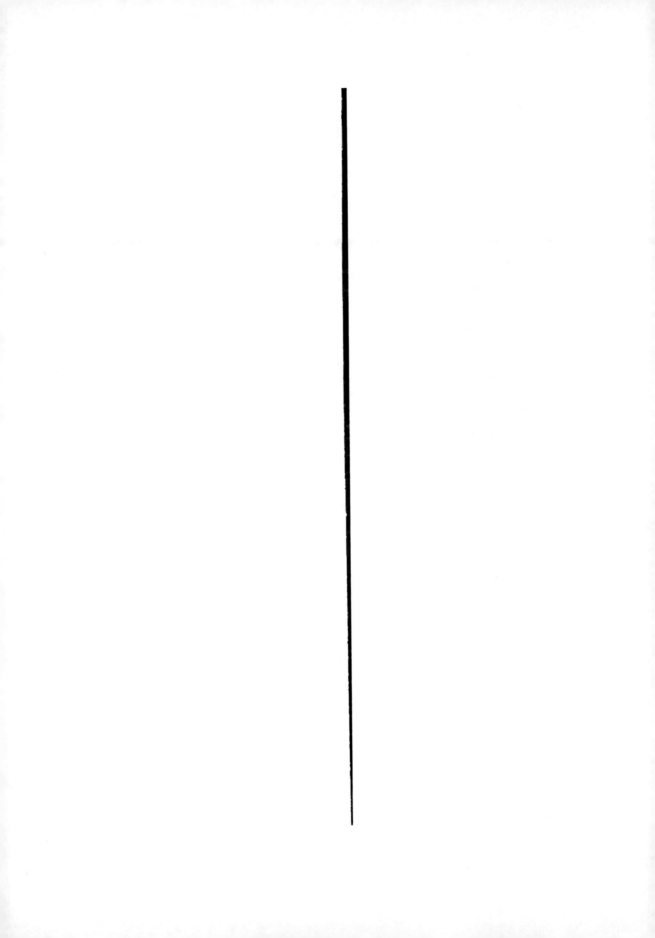

CPSIA information can be obtained at www.ICGtesting.com
Printed in the USA
BVOW01s1203080714

358479BV00022B/773/P